Brian Thorne, co-founder of The N
of Counselling, University of East
For me the reading of this diary ╷
experience. From my first meeting
aware of a man who, despite his eminence and achievements, was restless in spirit. I was also surprised by the number of occasions on which he sought me out in order, it seemed, to engage in philosophical and theological discussions. I remember lengthy conversations, for example, about French existentialism and the perversity of such Christian doctrines as Original Sin and punitive versions of the atonement. Reading Carl's China diary shows me that in some ways in 1978 I was encountering again the young Carl Rogers. There was the same desire to achieve clarity and honesty and a determination not to fudge important issues. There was the same impatience with theological doctrines which seemed either to run in the face of social injustice or to deny the essential validity of human nature. Above all there was the same passion for integrity and the loathing of hypocrisy. There were times indeed when I felt that Carl was in some ways putting me to the test. How, he seemed to be asking, had I succeeded in remaining a Christian without succumbing to illogicality, hypocrisy or, worst of all, a lust for spiritual power?

I like the young Carl of the diary as much as I warmed to the elderly 76 year old. The diary reveals the same openness of mind and heart and the same refusal meekly to accept authority that characterised the Carl I met in Madrid in 1978. There are, however, differences. The young Carl was reluctant, it seems, to speak before large groups and there are moments in the diary when it is clear that he finds it difficult to afford himself appropriate value and esteem. The Carl I met in his later years seemed to relish the chance to address a group and I do not recall any lapse into self-denigration. I sometimes wonder if Carl's rejection of Christianity was partly brought about by his fear that to remain a Christian would make it impossible for him to exercise his talents in the public arena without feeling either arrogant or power-seeking. Even more troubling is the thought that Carl believed that

Christianity proclaimed a view of human nature which would make it impossible for him ever to become truly self-loving. Such reflections induce feelings of melancholy which can be dispelled by the vision of a Carl who hugely enjoyed good food and drink and revelled in the congeniality of convivial company. This is the Carl who is happily present in his diary and was similarly at home in the restaurants of Spain in 1978. I am glad to have met the latter in the flesh and delighted now to encounter the former in the pages of this fascinating diary.

Martin van Kalmthout, Emeritus (Associate) Professor of Radboud University, Nijmegen, The Netherlands, writes:
The publication of this previously unpublished diary, written by Carl Rogers when he was only 20 years old, is certainly a major event for all students of Rogers' life and work. In addition, this diary is of extra value as it throws some light on Rogers' early struggle with religion, social justice and world peace. It also shows that the young Rogers had a long way to go to arrive at his radical views on all these issues. In this respect his relatively naive, but detailed, informational, and almost impersonal description of what he meets on his trip to China is moving. After reading the diary, many questions remain unanswered as to the personal details of his struggle. It is my hope that these questions will be answered in future publications of, for example, the letters he wrote in this period and later on, and perhaps other unpublished diaries.

Maureen O'Hara, Ph.D., Professor of Psychology, National University, La Jolla, California, USA, writes:
Ninety years after they were written, these pages sparkle with a freshness and frankness that even in the 21st century, seem contemporary. Much of the mature Rogers is already hinted at here. His empathy for his father's unspoken feelings as he readies to leave and exquisitely detailed observations of the trees, flowers, gardens, and livestock reveal an interest in nature that stayed with him throughout his life. But what stands out is the young Rogers' love of people – all kinds of people, who fascinate him in their uniqueness and diversity. Expressed in terms of his relationship with Christ, he is first saddened and ultimately

outraged about the injustices of a system that makes young girls work 14-hour shifts in bound feet, and that there were no old "riksha" pullers, noting that their toil as draft animals sends them to an early death. Nor does he deny his own and his comrades' complicity, reflecting on his own privilege as a wealthy Westerner and what his luxury costs the poor people he encounters. Here we see a young person who already identifies more with Christ than the Christian Church as he describes his deep solidarity with the oppressed and downtrodden and lays out his commitment to work toward their emancipation. His reflections, though avowedly Christian, transcend the doctrinal boundaries of any particular religious institution. The diaries are also astonishingly well written; the narrative is so compelling and detailed that I could not put it down. It was like hearing the future psychologist Carl Rogers whom I knew so well, in the clear thoughts, descriptions and reflections of the boy becoming man. This book is a genuine treasure on so many levels and should be read by person-centered therapists, psychologists, historians, and Christians who seek first-hand accounts of early 20th century missions to the East.

Carl Rogers

The China Diary

edited by
Jeffrey H.D. Cornelius-White

PCCS Books
Ross-on-Wye

First published 2012

PCCS BOOKS
2 Cropper Row
Alton Road
Ross-on-Wye
Herefordshire
HR9 5LA
UK
Tel +44 (0)1989 763900
contact@pccs-books.co.uk
www.pccs-books.co.uk

My Trip to China © The Estate of Carl Rogers
The Foreword © Natalie Rogers, 2012
All other matter © Jeffrey H. D. Cornelius-White, 2012

All rights reserved.
No part of this publication may be reproduced, stored in a retrieval system, transmitted or utilised in any form by any means, electronic, mechanical, photocopying or recording or otherwise without permission in writing from the publishers.

Carl Rogers: The China Diary

British Library Cataloguing in Publication Data.
A catalogue record for this book is available from the British Library.

ISBN 978 1 906254 50 6

Cover idea by Frances Fuchs, USA
Cover designed in the UK by Old Dog Graphics
Printed in the UK by Imprint Digital, Exeter

CONTENTS

List of Illustrations — i

Maps of the Journey — ii

Foreword by Natalie Rogers — v

Preface — xi

Introduction — 1

Cast of Characters — 11

"My Trip to China" — 21
    February — 21
    March — 45
    April — 90
    May — 119
    June — 143
    July — 162

Calendar — 177

Prominent Themes in the Diary — 195

References — 207

Index — 209

LIST OF ILLUSTRATIONS

Youthful Midwesterner: A young Carl in the U.S.	21
The North American delegation to China	31
Initial impressions of Japan: Sightseeing a Tokyo canal	53
"The shrines themselves are beautiful beyond description"	56
"There were also many Peking carts"	82
Procession in Peking	89
A man in Northern China: "The people are the real thing after all"	105
"The amount of starvation and malnutrition is something frightful"	129
Stairway to Shinto shrine	168
View of Mt. Fuji from a distance	170
Almost at the summit	171
Flag at the summit	171
A changed man: Carl after his return to the U.S.	175

Rogers' Route: February 15 – March 10 1922

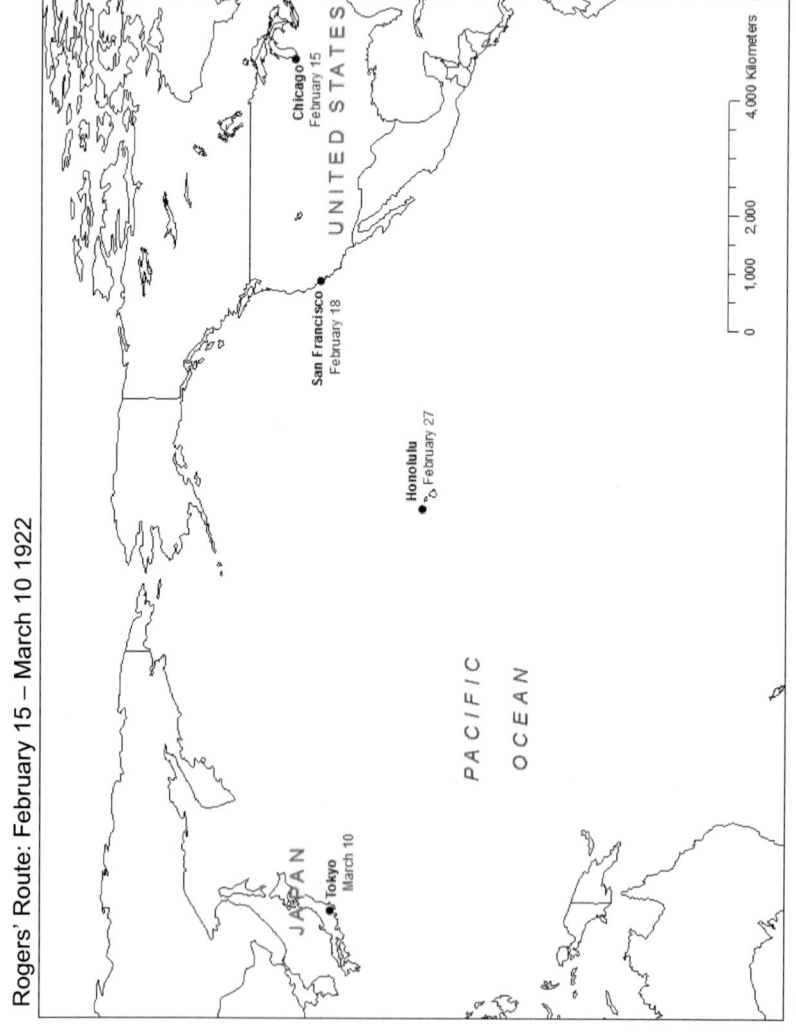

- Chicago, February 15
- San Francisco, February 18
- Honolulu, February 27
- Tokyo, March 10

Map made by Jeremy Thomas and Xiaomin Qiu. Data from ESRI.

MAPS OF THE JOURNEY

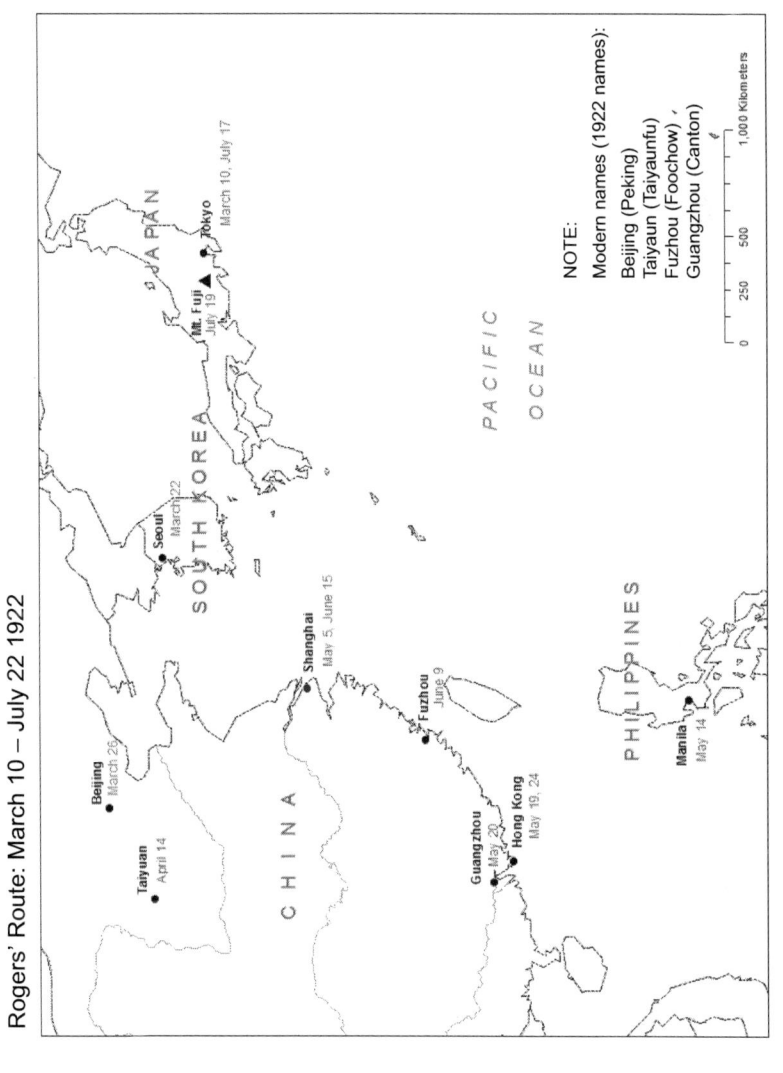

Rogers' Route: March 10 – July 22 1922

NOTE:
Modern names (1922 names):
Beijing (Peking)
Taiyaun (Taiyaunfu)
Fuzhou (Foochow)
Guangzhou (Canton)

Beijing — March 26
Taiyuan — April 14
Seoul — March 22
Shanghai — May 5, June 15
Fuzhou — June 9
Guangzhou — May 20
Hong Kong — May 19, 24
Manila — May 14
Mt. Fuji — July 19
Tokyo — March 10, July 17

Map made by Jeremy Thomas and Xiaomin Qiu. Data from ESRI.

FOREWORD

Reading Carl's *China Diary* is entering a doorway to his mind, heart and soul in his most formative year. In 1922 he was only 20. Through reading this diary it's been my privilege to get to know my father as an intellectually curious, insightful and observant youth, as he took off for a trip to the Orient. In this personal writing we see many of the characteristics that stayed with him for life: his interest in observing and documenting his experience and his interest in challenging his own and other people's beliefs in order to come to some new self-understanding.

The big question in my mind, as I read and re-read this diary is, "How did his journey to the Orient change young Carl's views and beliefs about Christianity?" I found myself wondering to what extent did this trip create the path between his faith in the Almighty to his faith in each human being.

The diary is a detailed description of his six-month travels from Chicago to San Francisco (by train) to Japan, Korea and China (by boat), as well as traveling in man-pulled rickshaws, buses, and doing a lot of hiking. All the time he documented what he saw, what he felt, and what he was thinking. He had a deep intuitive sense that this journey would be life altering. And indeed it was. He says as much on the first page.

> For the life of me, I cant realize that I am really off for six months of high adventure, with great experiences, and tremendous opportunities ahead of me. I cant help but wonder how much the trip will

change me, and whether the Carl Rogers that comes back will be more than a speaking acquaintance of the Carl Rogers that is going out. (February 15)

Carl could have taken a pen and a journal. Instead he lugged a heavy 25-pound typewriter in order to send documents home. Sitting on the train or up nights on the boat he recalled the sights, the people, his impressions and his shifting views of the world and his religious beliefs. It seems apparent that as he wrote he was talking to family and colleagues as well as to himself. This dedication to documenting and integrating his inner reactions with learning from life experiences continued until the end of his life and is one of the many reasons he was, and still is, widely read and appreciated.

As a student he was active in the University of Wisconsin Young Men's Christian Association (YMCA). His leadership skills were noted by the YMCA administrators, and he was one of ten students in the country selected to represent the United States at the World Student Christian Federation Conference in Peking, China in April 1922.

The Carl Rogers that left his home in Glen Ellen, a suburb outside of Chicago, was a young man having grown up in a strict, puritanical environment where the family gathered each morning for prayers and bible reading. The six children (Carl was the fourth) sat in the parlor taking turns reading bible paragraphs. After the reading each person knelt on the floor, hands folded on the chair in front of him, while mother or father gave the final blessing. After that was breakfast – starting with a prayer. Church was every Sunday, of course.

This was a household built on faith in God and with strict rules of moral conduct: no drinking, no smoking, no cards, no dancing and as far as I can tell no discussion of sexuality. The

FOREWORD

five boys rose early in the morning to feed the pigs and milk the cows. The daughter had indoor chores. Their farm was a "gentleman's" farm since Carl's father was a construction engineer doing big jobs building bridges and dams. Nevertheless, the parents thought it crucial for each child to take responsibility for some aspects of the large farm. After the chores were finished they usually walked the two miles to school. A strong work ethic pervaded the Rogers' household.

In the diary, Carl often speaks of his faith in God, his love for Jesus and the urgency for Christian morals to help shape a peaceful world.

> It isn't until one is facing a big job alone that one appreciates all that his faith in a Heavenly Father means to him. (February 15)
>
> I am sure that there is a God, who is a loving father. I am sure that Jesus Christ is my leader and Lord, and that I want to follow his principles of brotherhood. I am sure that his kingdom, as he calls it, offers the only solution for the problems of the world. (February 25)

These and other such statements amaze me! My brother, David, and I grew up in a home where our parents – Carl and Helen – did not *have* a bible, and I never heard either of them discuss God, Jesus, or faith in an Almighty. We didn't say prayers, nor did we ever go to church. I was left to figure out what I believed, on my own. If I had read this diary as a teenager I surely would have had a lot of questions to ask my father. (And my mother since she was more of a religious liberal than my dad.)[1] When

---
1. An in-depth analysis of this trip and Carl's shift to humanistic psychology can be found on pages 23–32 of Howard Kirschenbaum's (2007) extensive biography: *The Life and Work of Carl Rogers*. Ross-on-Wye, UK: PCCS Books.

vii

I read, "it was more imperative than ever that we set aside an unhurried time, each day, *for communion with God,* in order to renew our spiritual strength, to develop our power of vision, to develop our power for helping others …" (February 20th, italics mine), I asked myself, "Is this really my father?" At this stage of my life (I am 83) I feel a bit cheated that I did not get some element of this from him as I grew up. I consider myself spiritual (as did he in his later years) but *not willing to accept any dogma* regarding values and beliefs. Now that I write that, I realize I have heard him say the same thing.

I wonder, even now, how it could be that a man of such deep religious faith would close the door to initiating discussions with his family and colleagues about God and Jesus. (As a youngster, I always thought Jesus was a fairy tale made up to placate those who didn't have inner strength.) When he was asked, later in life, "Are you religious?" I remember him saying, "I am too religious to be religious." While I believe this to be true, to the questioner it could feel like a closed door. Why would he stop talking about such an important historic and world subject? Why wouldn't he share the story of his shifting beliefs the way he shared so many other personal beliefs? The answer to this question remains a mystery to me. Having left his strict home, which could be called a form of religious oppression, he may have closed the door tightly to that subject, not willing to engage in a dialogue regarding such a sensitive subject that would involve talking about his rejection of his parents' strong beliefs. Perhaps it lies in his fervent rejection of imposing religious beliefs on others.

As his daughter I am also intrigued with the personality characteristics, like leadership, that seemed evident at age 20 that were familiar to me as an adult friend and colleague.

FOREWORD

The fact that he was selected by a national YMCA committee to be one of ten U.S. students to represent the mission of the Y highlights the fact that he was already seen as a leader in the Christian Youth movement.

As he writes about the student meetings aboard the ship it seems that he took the lead in many discussions, partly because he was always eager to learn from others, a trait that continued through his life, and to stimulate his own thinking.

As the group traveled, Carl was often asked to give a talk to the various organizations telling the mission of the YMCA. He never says anything about being nervous or having to prepare for these, even when the audience was 600 people. His self-confidence when it came to intellectual ideas and his zeal for the mission apparently made it easy for him in these situations. On the final day of the international conference he wrote:

> I am afraid that I would have liked to differ again with the Ex Chancellor of the German Empire. He and I had a hard time agreeing, all the way thru. At 11:30 I had to speak for the American delegation, giving our message. (April 10)

It seems Carl was challenging the Ex-Chancellor throughout the conference! No wonder he was seen as a leader. He had the courage to confront his elders of high rank. (I guess I learned to question authority by osmosis.)

On April 16th he wrote:

> In spite of protest and vehement indignation, I had to lead the Easter service at the little Chinese Independent church here ... In the afternoon I had to talk to a

group of about 150 students from the different middle schools and colleges.

It is impressive that Carl's leadership was profoundly acknowledged as he was leaving China. Mr. Paul, the YMCA delegate from India, offered him a job if he would come to India immediately. Also, the U.S. delegates wanted him to return to China as a missionary after finishing college.

Carl's leadership abilities in his chosen field of psychology and psychotherapy brought him dozens of academic awards throughout his years. His initiative and pleasure in listening to and considering other people's views and *then* leading the way were a strong part of his early beginnings.

Overall, it has been a delight for me to be with my father in his youth, experience his energy and passion for life, and read about his intellectual fervor as I try to understand his early devotion to Christianity. During this journey he was also courting my mother, Helen, by mail, which is another story. (And a successful one!)

The Introduction that follows sets up the context of the diary. You can also follow his trip via the "Cast of Characters," "Calendar," and "Themes" chapters, and the maps provided. Best of all is to read the diary itself!

Natalie Rogers, Ph.D.
Sebastopol, California
www.nrogers.com

PREFACE

Carl Rogers is a giant in psychotherapy, humanistic psychology and related fields. "In both the 1982 and 2006 survey the single most influential psychotherapist – by a landslide – was Carl Rogers" (*Psychotherapy Networker*, 2007, para. 3). He won the most prestigious American Psychological Association awards for research and conducted the first empirical studies of psychotherapy (Kirschenbaum, 2007). Though a psychologist, Carl was in some ways the founder of the profession of counseling, bringing psychotherapy from psychiatry to psychology to other professions and helping to increase access to mental health services for hundreds of millions of people. Nearly every professional in training will watch one of his demonstration videos, read his works, or read about him in a textbook. Beyond psychotherapy, his ideas on facilitation have had enormous influence on the fields of management, mediation, and education (Cornelius-White & Motschnig-Pitrik, 2010).

However, equally important to his scientific and discipline influence was his stature as a person. It was his humanity that perhaps best encapsulates his enduring legacy. Carl was humble yet determined, kind yet assertive, empathic yet honest, and unconditional yet discerning. His quiet charisma is legendary and shared by the many people he touched and in turn, all of their facilitative interactions with others. Carl was a living example of the person-centered approach in action. He embodied warmth, empathy, and genuineness, the core

xi

conditions that facilitate beneficial development and characterize the person-centered approach.

During his life, Carl was in many ways an open book. He was transparent beyond most figures in the history of psychology, indeed the common usage of the word *transparence* as applied to personality and human interaction is largely due to his promotion of the concept in writing and life. However, Carl also valued his solitude and privacy and did not share many important aspects of his experience, either intentionally or because there is always more to a person and his or her life than one can directly share. Kirschenbaum (1979, 2007) has written the definitive biographies of Carl, although Carl wrote about a dozen autobiographical works; others have written biographies (e.g., Thorne, 2003), provided oral histories and videos, and authored biographical entries in textbooks and online are numerous. Kirschenbaum's (2007) recent and most comprehensive biography, Rogers and Russell's oral history (2002), and Natalie Rogers' *A Daughter's Tribute* (2003), a unique interactive media CD-ROM, were all released in the past decade and reveal several of these heretofore not commonly known aspects of Carl's experience and life. Nevertheless, relatively little has been written about Rogers during his transition from adolescence to adulthood despite that this life transition is central to many theories of identity development. *The China Diary* is perhaps the clearest and most thorough original source material for gaining an understanding of the budding man and his ideas.

Carl was prolific in his career, having authored more than 20 books and hundreds of articles. The comprehensive bibliography in Rogers and Russell (2002) shows that Rogers' first publication came out in 1922 concerning his trip to China (Rogers, 1922). This diary precedes that work and represents in a way his earliest and latest publication. *The China Diary* also makes clear that Rogers was a prolific writer even at 20 years old. He appeared to write hundreds of letters during the trip, edited a newsletter aboard the boat heading towards China, and, of course, kept the diary.

The diary is approximately 50,000 words and describes about two thirds of the days of a six-month, 172-day odyssey across the United States, the Pacific and through several Pacific Island and Far East mainland regions, including Hawaii, the Philippines, Japan, Korea, and especially China. It tells of where he went, when, for how long, why, and perhaps most importantly what he felt and made of the experience. It explores themes of religion, sociology, psychology, history, geography, and like any diary of course, personal revelations and identity development. The original diary now resides in the library archives in the Humanistic Psychology Special Collections at the University of California Santa Barbara. Excerpts appeared in the biography by Rogers and Russell, *Carl Rogers: The Quiet Revolutionary: An Oral History* (2002); the definitive biography, *The Life and Work of Carl Rogers* (Kirschenbaum, 2007); and the innovative multimedia CD-Rom *Carl Rogers: A Daughter's Tribute* (2003).

The Introduction provides some biographical context of the trip, the YMCA movement which he represented during the trip, the geopolitical context, and a brief overview of the plot of the diary. The "Cast of Characters" chapter provides short entries on persons of personal or historical importance during the trip. Several people Carl traveled with or interacted with were perhaps as influential as he was in their own fields, from which light the diary represents unique original source material.

The diary itself is preserved in its original form, without corrections for grammar, spelling or changes in English expression during the 90-year interval. Selected photos from the trip are interspersed to help the reader imagine beyond the words. The "Calendar" provides a day-by-day overview of the locations, activities, and themes Carl explored. It is complemented by maps (see pages ii and iii) that pinpoint the locations that Carl traveled during each month. The "Themes" chapter reflects on the major themes identified in the Calendar, including Carl's emerging existential faith, his openness to experience, his concern for social issues and peace, and the central role that his relational milieu played in fostering his own growth during this rich journey. The Foreword provides a daughter's personal view of her father in light of the revelations that the diary provided, including his stark avoidance of fostering an explicit religious upbringing despite a profound faith early in life, and how the trip resulted in the engagement and marriage of her parents.

The impetus for the publication of *Carl Rogers: The China Diary* has been years in the making but began in earnest at the 25th annual conference of the Association for the Development of the Person-Centered Approach in Rochester, New York in the summer of 2010. Natalie has a special place in her heart for the diary and was pleased to learn of Jef Cornelius-White and Wade Hannon's interest in it. Editing this book was facilitated by a summer fellowship awarded to Jef by the Graduate College of Missouri State University, the Person-Centered Press, a project of the Center for the Studies of the Person, and close collaboration between Natalie and Jef. Additionally, David Gartrell at the University of California Santa Barbara was helpful in providing photos and artifacts. Keith Wilson, Graduate Assistant in the Department of Counseling, Leadership and Special Education, Missouri State University was helpful in assembling elements of the "Calendar" and the "Cast of Characters." Thanks also go to Howard Kirschenbaum, Carl's official biographer, for his consultation, support, and reviews throughout the process.

We sincerely hope that you find gratitude and meaning as you journey with Carl across the seas!

INTRODUCTION

The diary was written by 20-year-old Carl Ransom Rogers during his six-month journey to the Far East in 1922, under the heading "My Trip to China." The never-before-published diary reveals intimate details of Rogers' religious faith, cross-cultural interactions, and emerging ideas on relationships, leadership, social injustice, and education. It is accompanied by supplemental features that help the reader to easily access the facts of his journey, explore its meanings, and share in the wonder of the journey that Carl himself in his later life called, "an absolutely mind-boggling experience" (Rogers & Russell, 2002, p. 60).

Biographical context[1]

Carl was born in 1902 in Oak Park, IL, outside Chicago. Unlike the other towering figures in the history of psychology, Rogers was American. In fact, his ancestors were American for centuries, with the oldest dating back to the 1630s on both maternal and paternal sides of his family tree. In some ways, one can see an American spirit of self-actualization and democratic interaction throughout Rogers' life and work, including in *The China Diary*.

Carl is often reported to have been overly sensitive, imaginative, and with fragile health during his early childhood.

---

1. Kirschenbaum's (2007) definitive biography of Carl Rogers provided the basis for much of this section.

He learned to read early and consistently enjoyed reading, but did not start school until he was nearly seven. Carl's family was strongly Christian and they prayed together in a family circle every morning. He did not appear to have close friends, but was in class with Helen Elliott (who became his wife) from the second grade. His family valued hard work and were reasonably affluent for the time. The family owned a suburban home and a farm with a large house, but sold the suburban house and moved to the farm full time when Carl was 13. Carl loved to play in the woods, became physically stronger, and near the time of their move he catalogued, bred, and passionately studied moths, becoming a bit of a biologist. He continued to be studious throughout his adolescence.

At the University of Wisconsin, Carl became more social. He participated in the YMCA and 4H (a youth organization, in Carl's time focused on agriculture and character building). He was selected as one of ten students to go the World Student Christian Federation conference in Peking (Beijing), China. On February 15, 1922, Carl embarked on his journey. While the conference lasted only about two weeks, Carl traveled for more than six months and visited several other countries and regions besides Peking, as described in the diary.

Despite his unusually resilient health during the trip, Carl became sick in the months after his return. He had to take a leave of absence from college. He had a business that helped him have financial security throughout his early 20s selling Chinese artifacts that he brought back with him and had mailed regularly to him. He decided to switch his major to history, believing that would help prepare him better for a life in the ministry.

He became engaged to Helen on October 22, 1922. They married in 1924 and remained so until her death in 1979, having two children, David (b. 1926) and Natalie (b. 1928). The Foreword to *The China Diary* highlights aspects of how Carl's trip related to his life as a father from the perspective of his daughter, Natalie.

After graduation, Carl moved to New York, over his parents' protestations, and began study at the Union Theological Seminary, perhaps the most liberal seminary of the day, which emphasized science, reason, and morality in addition to faith. He also took some psychology classes at Columbia, which was nearby. He was influenced by the ideas of Dewey and Kilpatrick at Columbia. He worked a year as a minister and then returned to university to be trained as a psychologist.

Carl's adult life as a psychologist is well known to many, and will only be covered briefly. After graduation from Columbia in 1931, he moved to Rochester where he worked with children. He made his first empirical studies and published his initial articles and books. In 1938, Carl was offered a position as a professor at Ohio University where he stayed until 1945. While in Ohio, he published one of his best-known works, *Client-Centered Therapy* (1951) and was elected President of the American Psychological Association (1946). The height of Carl's influence in academia and in empirical research came during the next two decades, while Carl was at the University of Chicago (from 1945 to 1957), and then the University of Wisconsin (from 1957 to 1963).

At the University of Chicago, he established the Chicago Counseling Center, a group of colleagues who would become highly influential for the next several decades. The group functioned in a uniquely egalitarian and nondirective way. They produced a high quality and quantity of psychotherapy research, including the first transcripts as well as sophisticated process and outcome studies. Highly influential offshoots of the person-centered approach – focusing, experiential therapy, nonviolent communication, filial therapy, play therapy, and other approaches – grew out of this flourishing group. Carl wrote his magnum opus theory statement during the mid 1950s which was then published in the Koch series, *Psychology: A Study of a Science* (Rogers, 1959).

At the University of Wisconsin, Carl was involved in a massive study of client-centered therapy with persons suffering from schizophrenia with Gendlin, Truax and Kiesler. Although there was evidence that the most successful cases did not complete final surveys, lowering results (Bozarth, 2011, personal communication), this study's write-up (Rogers, Gendlin, Kiesler, & Truax, 1967) and reception did not have the resounding support for client-centered therapy that other studies had revealed. Also, Carl had some conflict in his dual appointment in psychology and psychiatry and did not seem to flourish or enjoy himself as he had in Chicago.

Carl moved to La Jolla, California and working at the Western Behavioral Sciences Institute from 1963–1968. There, he established the Center for the Studies of the Person (CSP). Carl focused on large and small group work. He and his groups were the subject of *Journey into Self*, an Academy Award-winning documentary (Rogers, 1968). While person-centered educational and political research dates back to the late 1930s (Cornelius-White & Harbaugh, 2010), Carl focused more attention on these subjects during this period with such works as *Freedom to Learn* (1969, 1983, 1994) and *Carl Rogers on Personal Power: Its Inner Strength and Its Revolutionary Impact* (1977). He also published *On Becoming a Person* (1961) and *A Way of Being* (1980), books that broadened his appeal to lay people while further elaborating his ideas.

INTRODUCTION

In his final decade, Carl became increasingly concerned with peace and group conflict issues. The Peace Project was an initiative of the Center for the Studies of the Person. In July 1986, the first Cross-Cultural Workshop in Szeged, Hungary occurred. It sponsored the Central American Challenge, a workshop in Rust, Austria, involving several prominent political, religious and business people, in November 1986. In the fall of 1987, there were meetings in the USSR. He also led peace workshops in Northern Ireland, South Africa, and elsewhere.

Carl became more spiritual in his writings during his final years. He wrote more about transpersonal characteristics of facilitative relationships, especially as related to his concept of presence. He traveled and interacted with spiritual healers and leaders and seemed to be more open to less empirically grounded views of reality. While dramatically different than his dogmatic upbringing and evangelical youth, his return to the transcendent in his later life is an intriguing aspect of his biography given his zeal for faith as seen in *The China Diary* in his young adult years.

The religious and higher education context of the YMCA and WSCF[2]

John Mott was the National Secretary of the Intercollegiate Young Men's Christian Association (YMCA) from 1888–1915, a period which was characterized less by the Y's pursuit of student salvation than by the development of character and service and it became an integral part of higher education. John Mott was a frequent companion to Carl during this trip and it is obvious that Mott was a significant influence on Carl given

---

2. Much of this section references Setran's (2007) history of the YMCA.

how he discussed him. Although the conference had delegates from around the world, providing rich cross-cultural interaction at a time between the World Wars and other important geopolitical events, Mott was nevertheless probably the most influential member, as past National Secretary of the YMCA and the chair of the World Student Christian Federation, from 1895–1920. The "Cast of Characters" chapter provides more information on John Mott as well as David Porter, another frequent companion and Secretary of the YMCA from 1915–1934.

During its heyday, nearly 30 percent of all American male college students belonged to the Y. "Student Affairs" departments on college campuses did not yet exist but instead were largely run through Y projects. In the late 1920s and 1930s under Porter, the near monopoly on student activities that the Y had began to fade as did the religious nature of higher education, but the Y's progressive message of infusing social and ethical principles continued through increasingly secular means. Setran (2007) wrote,

> Fostered by a new affiliation with the forces of liberal Protestantism and progressive education, the organization substituted attempts to secure Christian character and service with aspirations toward the construction of a new Christianized world. Dropping much of the traditional program and adopting instead a Christ-inspired devotion to a democratic social order, students were directed toward a thoughtful engagement with vexing social issues of war, race, and economic justice. (p. 6)

In some ways, the journey of the YMCA towards a more embodied, socially engaged and humanistic faith and away from evangelical dogma finds a parallel in Carl's own evolving faith. Setran (2007) calls Carl Rogers' own journey a "helpful case study of emerging ideals" of the YMCA (p. 203).

Historical context of East Asia and Western nations[3]

Before the 1800s, Western nations had relatively little influence in East Asia. However, with the aim of forcing the Chinese to allow free trade, Britain began to import large quantities of opium into China, leading to the First Anglo-Chinese War, which China lost in 1842, signing a treaty giving Hong Kong to the British, as well as special trading rights. During the Taiping Rebellion (1850–1864), one of the bloodiest of internal civil wars, costing millions of lives, the Chinese Government also faced the British and French in the Second Anglo-Chinese or Second Opium War, again ending in defeat for China, which led to further special treaties in 1860 with Great Britain and France, the U.S. and Russia. China lost a war with Japan in 1895, which gave Korea full independence from China, and secured special trading rights for Japan. The Boxer Rebellion occurred during the subsequent decade, where many Westerners and Christians in China were killed, before an alliance of eight Western nations, including Russia and Japan, crushed it. Western nations continued to hold significant if declining influence in the region into the 1930s.

The Republic of China was formally created in 1912 among southern and central provinces, separating them from the rule of the Manchus in the north, but this was quickly followed by multiple war lords seizing power and a civil war that was widespread in 1922, the year that Carl traveled. The

---

3. This section draws extensively upon Hutchings' (2001) history of modern China.

Soviet Union was established in 1922, and Chinese Communist groups became increasingly influenced by Russia, who helped them to consolidate and then oppose central control. By 1928, central control was once again established, but armed conflicts between Communists and Nationalists continued, with the Communists gaining control of the South-Central regions of China. During this period, Japan opportunistically occupied Manchuria and adjacent regions up into Mongolia. The Japanese controlled much of Eastern China by 1938. China sided with the Allies during World War II, however, it was very weakened by the conflicts between Nationalists and Communists and with Japan. Nationalist armies retreated to Taiwan and civil war again broke out at the end of World War II continuing until 1949 when Communist Chairman Mao Zedong (Tse-Tung) formerly established the People's Republic of China. China experienced extensive economic development during the next decade, but oppressive policies and the Cultural Revolution of 1966 brought more violence. Stability was again achieved in the 1970s when China and the Western nations established full diplomatic relations, which, not without tension, have continued largely until today.

Overview of
Carl Rogers: The China Diary

In a nutshell, Rogers begins as a farm boy in February 1922, travels by train to San Francisco, boards a ship heading towards the Orient, and finds that he has sea legs, better sea legs than his travel companions. He visits Hawaii, Japan, Korea and Manchuria before attending the World Student Federation Conference beginning in late March, six weeks after the commencement of his journey.

INTRODUCTION

At this point, although nearly half of the diary has been written, the majority of his trip, and much of his inner journey, is yet to come. He becomes a self-directed and cooperative leader. He is outspoken as a diplomat and makes many speeches. His faith deepens, broadens and becomes more relational and existential as he encounters so many people. He has an adventure on the high seas involving proximity to pirates and typhoons.[4]

One might say that the climax of the diary falls on what Rogers calls "Meridian Day," "the first day that I have ever lived that has had no date." It is in this entry for July 26–27 that he describes having climbed Mt. Fuji in the week previous. This entry has been perhaps most cited in published works. Though not long per se, the description of the climb is the longest of a single activity within the diary (more than 1000 words) and narrates the adventure and activity far more than the ideas or abstractions as compared to other entries. Nevertheless, Carl imbues the words with emotion, and it is easy for the reader to share in the experience and imagine oneself on the journey.

The final entry provides what might be called the denouement, highlighting what the trip has meant to him and foreshadowing his life to come. He describes three things of import concerning his journey home: "thinking and meditating over my experiences and impressions of China and the East," "thinking about what part I shall take, and what attitude I shall take toward the Y work at school next fall," and "some mighty concentrated thinking for myself," particularly related

---

4. Of historical interest is that a couple of weeks after Carl is in Swatow, the city was destroyed by one of the worst typhoons in recorded history in which 100,000 persons perished. The city has grown to 5 million people from the 15,000 people left in August 1922 (Hutchings, 2001).

to mutually sought-out interactions with Dr. H. B. Sharman. The very last sentence of the diary claims that Sharman "is the most stimulating man I have ever been with, and it has been a wonderful opportunity to be with him." The phrase "be with" as the final statement of the diary seems significant. He did not say "discuss," as he had 23 other times, but instead "be with," alluding to the prominence that a way of being would have in his most mature works and philosophy.

Carl stated his future purpose thus: "My main job when I get back, as I see it, is to get the men to think – and when I have gotten them to thinking a little bit, then to get them to think some more – and some more! … to make men thoroly uncomfortable, to drag them out and make them think." With a cliffhanger ending, Carl stated, "I have just three little things that I myself want to do – just three things, and if I can do them they will really count for something, but I'm not even telling now what they are." One wonders whether huge life-altering decisions were reached in the final days of his trip, such as his career change toward ministry and its eventual evolution toward psychology, or proposing to Helen, leading to the creation of his enduring family and their contributions.

CAST OF CHARACTERS

Carl Rogers put relationship at the center of focus for psychotherapy, learning, and other human endeavors in which fostering growth or change is of significance. Likewise, one of Carl's most enduring contributions is a particular way of being in relationships. Carl's own relationships during his journey are vital to understanding the diary and the development of his personhood and ideas. Carl first provided a thorough description of several people, including all of the major players except H. B. Sharman, in the February 21 diary entry. His many relationships provided the "forge of discussions" that "hammered out" his faith and growth as a person (March 5).

By definition, a diary is a personal record of experiences and observations. However, *The China Diary* is not just the story of one man's journey; it truly has an ensemble cast. There are several people that Carl explicitly described as noteworthy to him, many more with whom he interacts but mentions in passing, and still others who are not described but are of large importance to Carl during his trip. Likewise, the diary represents an original source on the personalities of the leaders of Christian missionary work, the YMCA, and to a lesser extent theology and international politics.

The major players: Mott, Porter, King, LaTourette, and Sharman

Carl described a few people several times or in such a way that it is clear they have been essential to his experience during the trip, and potentially in an enduring way. Interestingly, each of these persons is a person of historical interest beyond the diary and worthy of a biography in their own right. These five men facilitated the development of Carl's identity, way of being, and ideas about religion, leadership, learning, and personal growth at the start of his adulthood. Perhaps the most important to Carl was John R. Mott.

John R. Mott (Carl calls him "Mott")
Carl's initial impressions of John Mott were that he "has a commanding personality. His talk was quiet, but very forceful" (February 20), and "only high mucky-mucks sit at Motts table" (February 22). However, he quickly warmed to him and then revered him for the rest of the trip, "The more I see of that man the more I admire him and the better I like him. He surely is a fine executive" (February 23). Carl frequently mentioned how much Mott's sermons, speeches, and discussions inspired him. He becomes more informal, and certainly more free with Mott, though possibly never as much as with some of his companions. Carl appeared to look up to Mott, perhaps more than anyone else, as an ideal of leadership and thought.

During 1922 when Carl traveled with him, Mott was perhaps the most prominent member of the World Student Christian Federation (WSCF), having served as General Secretary of the WSCF from 1895–1920 and National Secretary of the Intercollegiate YMCA from 1988–1915 (Setran, 2007). Mott also presided over the 1910 World Missionary Conference, which launched the modern ecumenical movement, or movement towards unity and cooperation between all Christian churches. After the 1922 trip, Mott continued his international work and was awarded the Nobel Peace Prize in 1946. He also wrote extensively and was considered a "world citizen" (Hopkins, 1979). After Mott, Dave Porter is perhaps the next most frequently discussed person and somewhat of a less formal chap in Carl's view.

David R. Porter (Carl calls him "Porter" and then eventually "Dave")

Carl looked forward to seeing Porter in San Francisco before they boarded the boat. His initial impressions of Porter were that he was a "likeable middle aged fellow … and very easy to get acquainted with" (February 21). Carl writes about Porter frequently but does not reveal much about how his ideas may have influenced him or the nature of their relationship (other than it being warm).

Dave Porter was Secretary of the YMCA from 1915–1934 and helped to foster the Y's social justice agenda, and initiatives related to war and pacifism, racial equality and economic justice. It was under his leadership that the YMCA both peaked and declined in influence in secondary and higher education settings. Like all of the other "major players," Porter wrote several books on religion, though he did not hold professorships (Setran, 2007). While Porter was a stabilizing force, Professor King was in even closer proximity to Carl and a person with whom Carl expanded his understanding of cultural similarities and differences.

Willis J. King (Carl calls him "Professor King" or "Willis")

During the month it took to travel to the Far East, Carl's roommate was Professor King. King was African American, a characteristic that was noteworthy during that time and place. For a white and black to room together was unusual as Carl recalled late in his life (Rogers & Russell, 2002). Carl initially described King saying, "He surely is a white man under his coal black skin" (February 22). Likewise, Carl commented on how many of the persons with whom Carl interacted, both conference delegates and peasants alike, had never seen or interacted with a person with dark skin. Indeed, Carl himself grew from the time he spent with King, realizing that a person of color can achieve success and stretching the cross-cultural Christian message, "The people around us always get a liberal education watching Willis" (May 11).

Willis King was the black students' representative for the WSFC. He was a Professor of Theology and a President of three Universities between 1918 and 1944. After that King was a bishop of the United Methodist Church presiding over the Liberia Conference from 1944–1956 and the New Orleans Area from 1956–1960. He continued speaking engagements and writing until his death in 1976, serving at that time as the oldest living Methodist bishop. In the 1920s he wrote *The Negro in American Life* and in the 1940s, *Christian Bases of World Order* (Sherer, n.d.). Carl became even closer with one other professor, traveling more extensively and describing with more fondness and depth: Ken LaTourette.

Kenneth Scott LaTourette (Carl calls him "Ken")
Carl spent considerable time with Ken throughout his whole trip, but it was in April through July that he traveled in a smaller group and interacted with Ken extensively every day. Ken became a great asset to Carl in that the two found many adventures together, and Ken's extensive connections afforded Carl to meet many new people he would later reflect a great deal on. Carl admired the way he interacted with others, encouraging their honest sharing. For example, when the two of them were talking with Colonel Johnston, assistant to

General Wood, the Governor of the Philippines at the time, Carl described Ken thus, "At first he [Col. Johnston] wasnt inclined to really express his opinion, but Ken very skilfully drew him out, and before he ended, he was certainly frank enough" (May 17). After a "startling" and "sincere" conversation, Colonel Johnston got the idea to check and see if General Wood could talk with them, which he could. This allowed Carl yet another opportunity to interact with a leader and confront difficult social and political realities.

LaTourette was a professor at Yale Divinity School beginning in 1921 until 1953 and served in several roles including Chair of the Department. He was an expert and wrote over 80 books on China and Japan in additional to World Christianity and mission work. LaTourette was a president of the American Historical Association and the American Baptist Convention, and several buildings and initiatives still bear his name. He continued writing as Emeritus faculty till his death in 1968 (Anderson, 1999). One final scholar had a large influence on Rogers during this time, H. B. Sharman.

H. B. (Henry Burton) Sharman (Carl calls him "Dr. Sharman")
Carl only described Sharman in the final paragraph of the diary. However, the way with which Carl described Sharman reveals his importance: "He is the most stimulating man I have ever been with" (July 30). During the final weeks of his journey, Carl wrote only this one entry, and he described that he was interacting extensively and daily with Sharman. Likewise, 63 years later, Carl described the importance of his relationship with Sharman as much as any other person, stating, "I was very much helped by a man named Henry Sharman … He's one of these teachers who was a good enough teacher that I

never was *quite* sure what he believed" (Rogers & Russell, 2002, p. 61). Carl admired his neutrality and openness in not pushing his own beliefs, an educational philosophy he would articulate at length in *Freedom to Learn* (1969, 1983) and other works. Nevertheless, one can know from the diary itself, Carl's own reflections on his importance 63 years later, and the many writings of Sharman, that Sharman was influential in helping Carl understand Jesus as a man rather than (only) a deity. It was this human quality that became more inspiring to Carl over time. It inspired Carl to live out his existential faith and fostered the foundation of humanism as the third major force in the history of psychology.

H. B. Sharman was a Christian philosopher and liberal evangelical. He became involved in the ministry in 1893 through the Student Volunteer Movement after being discovered by John R. Mott. He was a doctoral student and then served as a lecturer at the University of Chicago Divinity School between 1900 and 1909. Sharman attended the WSCF on behalf of the Student Christian Movement of Canada. Sharman taught extensively in California, Canada, China and other locations and became an authority on the gospels, approaching them in a uniquely Socratic way. He had several famous students (Setran, 2007).

The supporting cast: Fellow travelers, the masses, and world leaders

In addition to substantial depth, Carl's relational milieu during his trip had extraordinary breadth. He mentioned an amazing 113 distinct persons. Some of these are people he discussed multiple times and with whom he became quite close. Sixty years later, Carl remembered some by name and with continuing emotional resonance (Rogers & Russell, 2002). Others he mentioned once, but sometimes they were leaders and distinguished people during their time or across history.

Finally, another indicator of the breadth of Carl's relational climate is the vast groups with which he interacted. He attended two large conferences, (the World Student Christian Federation Conference and later the first Chinese Christian Conference) with hundreds of participants from many regions, countries, and continents. Carl was one of the 10 persons on the Executive Committee and one of 55 on the General Committee of the WSCF. He gave speeches to thousands of local persons and missionaries while sightseeing and touring factories, hospitals, universities, schools, and a prison. While late in life Carl felt "the arrogance of trying to tell Chinese students what they should know or believe really embarrasses me now," at the time it afforded Carl a tremendous opportunity to engage with large numbers of people (Rogers & Russell, 2002, p. 59).

A few people he described but were not discussed as major players in his relational milieu included:

- Helen Kasbeer, another student delegate from Wisconsin, with whom Carl regularly interacted and recalled 63 years later with fondness (Rogers & Russell, 2002).
- Austin Case, another student delegate from Washington whom Carl befriended and shared several adventures.
- Ex-Chancellor Michaelis of Germany, with whom Rogers repeatedly disagreed on issues of Christianity and war/pacifism during WSFC General Committee debates.
- Leonard Wood, Governor General of the Philippines, with whom Carl talked informally during his visit.

- John Lawrence "Jack" Childs, a local secretary of the YMCA in China and in 1931 a Columbia University professor following John Dewey's retirement, who Carl heard speak at the WSCF Conference.
- John Hays Geldart, a secretary of the YMCA in China from 1911–1925, with whom Carl interacted and is described frequently in the diary.
- The Mayor of Seoul and the head of the Foreign Relations Department of Korea, whose names were not given and were not found in online records, and Chief Justice Watanabe whom Carl met while touring Korea.
- Dr. H. T. Hodgkin, a prominent missionary with whom Carl toured a prison, several Chinese cities, at times by motorcycle, and who provided much enjoyment.

The absent persons: Carl's parents and Helen Elliott

In describing his experience in China late in life, Carl recalled,

> It was just an absolutely mind-boggling experience, and I evidently was very open to it. And I think one reason was that all contact with home and other background was cut off ... So I was totally free to think my own thoughts. (Rogers & Russell, 2002, p. 60)

In other words, Carl's relational milieu did not consist only of the daily, intimate time with renowned Christian mentors or the thousands of others that Carl interacted; those closest to him back home had a pivotal role through their absence. In the case of his parents, the absence appeared to allow him a freedom of exploration. Carl's parents had more traditional, conservative views on religion and social issues which contrasted with Carl's own emerging views.

In the case of Helen, absence made his heart grow fonder. Carl had proposed to Helen before he left on the trip. She had reservations, and wanted to delay before giving him an answer. Helen had made Carl promise that he would not write love letters, but Carl broke that promise. On February 20, less than a week into his trip before he boards the ship, he seemed to be hoping to hear from Helen when he wrote,

> I surely have been fortunate as to mail since I have been here. I have received 8 letters and one night letter from home in the two days I have been here. Now just one more letter, providing it is the right one, and I will be satisfied.

He did not discuss Helen Elliott directly in his diary, but he did correspond regularly. Carl recalled "it was really a very romantic time for me" (Rogers & Russell, 2002, p. 79). He wrote her love poetry and letters both while away and when he returned. For example, Carl wrote to her during this time period, "I'm so thankful I have a girl whom I can love in so many ways …" and "I had the most glorious time last night, although I thought my heart would burst for wanting you" (Kirschenbaum, 2007, pp. 39–40). On October 22, the girl he knew and liked since second grade said yes.

Central to understanding the role of these relationships is to understand that Carl sent selections from his diary and wrote letters routinely back home, "I was writing home very excited letters with all these new ideas – how marvelous they were, and weren't they great and so forth" (Rogers & Russell, 2002, p. 60). In this way, his parents and Helen were very much a part of his trip. However, equally important is the delay by which this correspondence transpired. It would take two to three months for a letter to be received back home and a return letter read by Carl. In other words, it was the chance to interact but with space that allowed him the opportunity to change and grow. Samples of correspondence are housed with the original diary in the Humanistic Psychology Special Collections at the University of California Santa Barbara.

MY TRIP TO CHINA

Wed, Feb 15

Youthful Midwesterner: A young Carl in the U.S.

This last day at home was much easier than I had dared to hope. Tuesday was really very much more gloomy and homesick than today. Of course there were other reasons on Tuesday, too. My trunk was sent off, my grips packed, and I was ready to go by noon, so in the afternoon, Sis, John, and I went skating. Father came home early and the way he acted would have been funny, if I hadnt known that half of the things he did were done simply to cover up the fact that he hated like the dickens to see

---

Note: As mentioned in the Preface, this is a transcript of the diary, without corrections for grammar or spelling.

me go. He couldnt turn around without thinking of something else that I ought to take with me, even at the last moment trying to give me six numbers of "Asia," on the ground that I would need something to read on the train, altho he knew that I had three books and several magazines. At 8:51 the Overland Limited stopped at Wheaton to pick me up and I told them all goodby for the last time in some months. I read for about an hour and a half after I got on board, finishing about 110 pages of Prof. Ross' book on "The Changing Chinese." This kept me from thinking about anything else which might not have been so pleasant.

For the life of me, I cant realize that I am really off for six months of high adventure, with great experiences, and tremendous opportunities ahead of me. I cant help but wonder how much the trip will change me, and whether the Carl Rogers that comes back will be more than a speaking acquaintance of the Carl Rogers that is going out. As long as I have a will of my own, I guess it is up to me whether the trip changes me for better or for worse. I certainly feel rather small and alone starting out on a trip like this. It isn't until one is facing a big job alone that one appreciates all that his faith in a Heavenly Father means to him. At a time like this I forget all the doubtful questions of my religion, all the minor disputable points, and cut below that to the vital faith in a living Master which is so much more important. I think that the reason I felt rather disappointed with the discussion Helen and I had on religion, as I analyzed it later, was that we both of us limited ourselves to the negative side of our religion. We didnt hesitate to say what we did not believe, but we were short on saying what we were sure of. Our religion is worse than useless, if it is only a negative thing, for by its very nature it ought to be the most positive and compelling force in our lives. According to my firm conviction, it doesnt make much difference what we do not believe, even though it is an old church doctrine, but it does make a tremendous difference what we DO believe, and believe in strongly enough to make our lives conform to our beliefs. Well, this is a long way off from my trip, and I will try not to stray this way again.

Thursday, Feb 16

I slept like a log last night, and was up fairly early this morning. In fact I was the last one to bed and the first one up, and have finished about 150 pages of a book on Japan as well as having looked at the scenery a lot and read several descriptive pamphlets on the scenery we are passing through. We woke up in Iowa but at 9:30, just out of Council Bluffs, we crossed the muddy Missouri, and found ourselves in Omaha, Nebraska. We have been traveling all day through the plains country, not as flat or as desolate as the Dakota prairies, but rather monotonous, nevertheless. It is a country of great level corn fields and meadows, with the farm houses few and widely scattered. We are following the valley of the Platte River, and catch a glimpse of it every now and then, to the south of us. At North Platte, in about an hour, we will have the unusual opportunity of living the same hour through twice, as we set our watches back an hour. Before night we will be in Colorado, and tomorrow morning the scenery ought to begin to be interesting.

There are some fairly interesting people on the train. The man who sleeps over me is a Chinese or Japanese, I cant tell which, and I have such an awful time trying to understand him, and he gets so scared when I talk to him, that my attempts at conversation have rather gone for nothing. There are two people, a man and a woman, who are evidently taking a Cook's tour for Japan and China. From what I have overheard, they were going to sail on the "Taiyo Maru" but they have been changed to another ship.

I nearly got left at Grand Island this noon. We stopped for five minutes and I figured that it would probably be a little more than five minutes, so I went into the lunch room and started to eat a sandwich and a glass of milk. I can now testify to the fact that it is a heartrending feeling to see your train pulling out without you. Luckily, I caught it, and doubt whether I will cut the corners as close again.

Friday, Feb 17

Before night last night we were in the foothills, and undoubtably passed through some very interesting country in the neighborhood of Cheyenne, but I was sound asleep. This morning it was snowing quite hard, and we could only see the bald, high hills thru a veil of driving snow. The fact that we cold only see them dimly, made them seem larger than they really are. After a while it cleared off, and we passed thru miles of foothills, curiously wrought by the action of water, and covered with sagebrush and little, gnarled, twisty, deformed scrub pines. On these hills we saw again and again herds of cattle, sheep and horses, without any protection whatsoever, but browsing in the sagebrush, or sometimes around a small haystack. Later we came into real mountains, great rugged forms, high against the sky, with sheer rock faces which stood out black against the white snow background. Unfortunately it was too cloudy to take any pictures.

We passed the highest point of our journey last night near Cheyenne, when we were 7000 feet higher than Chicago, and all this afternoon we have been coming down. Finally we reached Ogden and then we started to cross the Great Salt Lake, going over 30 miles on a causeway straight across the lake. It surely is a remarkable engineering feat, but not so awfully exciting to look at. The mountains around the northern brim of the lake were beautiful, tho. I had no idea it was so mountainous anywhere in Utah. All this afternoon we have been passing through wonderful mountain scenery. It has been cloudy almost all the time and many of the dark old mountains have been wreathed or belted with soft, fleecy clouds. There was one old mountain late this afternoon, lit up by the sun shining through a rift in the grey, with a long cottony cloud right across its side halfway up, that I don't think I will soon forget.

We are climbing again now into the Sierras, and tomorrow will undoubtably be even more beautiful than today, as we descend into the sunny plains of California.

I have to sort of pinch myself every now and then to believe that I am really on my trip, and that I have left home for six months. It doesnt seem real to me yet, any more than it did when I told them goodby.

Saturday, Feb 18

This morning we woke up at Truckee, Cal. The snow was nearly a foot deep, and the town and the mountains looked very wintry in their white blanket of snow. We were really in the Sierras now and the mountains were fine and sparsely covered with pine and firs. We passed the summit of the Sierras about 8 A.M. and started coming down for the second time. We passed thru about forty miles of snowsheds, which had only little peepholes every now and then, giving one a most tantalizing view of the wonderful ravines and canyons below, almost hidden by the heavy wet snow which was falling. At Blue Canyon the view was magnificent. We were more than halfway up the side of the mountain which sloped away almost perpendicularly to the tiny thread of a river which one could see hundreds of feet below. The mountainsides were covered with fine green pine trees decked and festooned with the snow. These great deep ravines, with their steep woodes sides, certainly get me. I love them.

With almost unbelievable rapidity we passed out of the region of snow and soon were in the placer mining country, the scene of so many of the successes and failures of the "49ers." In some places, whole hills and mountains have been literally turned upside down and washed for their hidden treasure.

After the mining region, the orchards started. All sorts of ordinary fruits - apples, pears, etc, - and many which were new to me - orange, olive, fig, and grape orchards and vineyards. The olive trees are beautiful when well taken care of. It seemed awfully funny to see all the green grass and trees in leaf, etc, especially after the early part of the morning spent in a bad snow storm. We were rapidly descending all the time, and soon were in the famous Sacramento valley, braod, quite level, and certainly very fertile. From what I have seen of California today, I like it most excellently, except for the fact that it rained or was cloudy all day and I was unable to get any pictures.

At Port Acosta this afternoon we had the novel experience of riding on a train ferry, for about a mile. The train was run right onto the ferry and off we sailed as big as life. They say the ferries are the largest in the world and I believe them. From Port Acosta it wasnt such a very long ride into Oakland where I took the ferry for Frisco. About an hour before I got off, however, I made the acquaintance of Jean Kennedy, the Mt. Holyoke girl who is a delegate to the conference. I had long ago picked her as the best looking girl on the train, but had no idea that she was going to China. She seems to be a nice girl and it seemed good to get in touch with somebody else who is going to the Conference.

When I arrived in Frisco, I went up to the Y where I found that Mott and Porter have arrived, but I couldnt get ahold of them, because they were not at the hotel where they were supposed to be. I have a nice little room here at the Hotel Stewart, and think that I will stay here unless they kick me out for making too much noise on my typewriter.

Sunday, Feb 19

This morning I wrote a couple of letters, and then went to a big Congregational church on the corner of Post and Mason. The minister and the sermon were most peculiar. He believed most ardently in spiritualism, and put forth all the ideas of Sir Oliver Lodge and others. His sermon was almost spooky, it seemed to me, as for instance when he was trying to convince us that all the atmosphere was filled with living spirits and ghosts. There may be something to all this "psychic" stuff, but I am afraid that he didnt convince me of it. I did have to smile, though, to think of all the differing ideas and beliefs and doctrines that pass in the name of Christianity. I wonder if Christ would recognize his own ideas in the mass of stuff that goes under his name. I guess that he could still find the central truths that he tried to teach, but he would have to hunt a long ways, and throw away a lot of dusty old doctrines before he found them.

In the afternoon, in spite of the rain, I took a sightseeing bus to Oakland and Berkeley. First we went across the big ferry to Oakland, past Alcatraz Is., where the penitentiary is located, and past Goat Is., where there is a big naval training station. There were four battle cruisers anchored in the harbor, too. We drove thru Oakland into Berkeley, and up to the University. I was disappointed in the campus. They have some pretty buildings, especially their great Campanile tower, but their buildings are all just splotched around on a campus, which by its rolling topography, might have been made a real beauty spot. I can't see how they can accomodate 12,000 students in those buildings, either. I think that our guide stretched that a little. From the Californians I have met, I should say that any Californian would stretch anything to make California seem a little greater. The best piece of provincialism I heard, tho, was from a man on the train who had been abroad and done a good deal of traveling and certainly ought to have lost his provincialism. He said that he had seen the Alps and that they couldnt hold a candle to the Sierras along the eastern edge of California that we were passing through. I didnt have the heart to tell him that even the Canadian Rockies had it all over his California mountains. To him everything that was of California was perfect. It simply could not be improved upon. To get back to sightseeing, tho. After Berkeley we went through Claremont, passing all the fawncy homes of the ultra rich. The trees and flowers here were the best we had seen. We saw some roses, a few iris and a great many smaller flowers in bloom. The magnolia and palm trees are very pretty, too. On the whole, I like Frisco very much. It still has a little of a western flavor, for it hasnt entirely gotten to the stage of a full grown big city, and it is, I think, quite a pretty city. It is a great city for flowers. Even on the street corners, they sell lovely flowers of all kinds. They have a regular outdoor flower market at the corner of Kearney and Market.

In the evening I wrote home, and then tried to read, but I couldnt stay awake, so I went to bed and slept like a log.

Monday, Feb 20

After breakfast i went to the office of the T.K.K. Line, and got my ticket for my cabin, Cabin 209, on the port side, I think, and right amidships. I also found three letters there for me, one of them from Dad Wolf. I surely have been fortunate as to mail since I have been here. I have received 8 letters and one night letter from home in the two days I have been here. Now just one more letter, providing it is the right one, and I will be satisfied.

After getting my ticket I went up to the Chinese consulate and got my passport vised. Then, since I never go the same route twice, if I can help it, when I am in a strange city, I turned up the hill, to come back a different way. Imagine my delight when I ran plump into Chinatown. I accordingly took myself on a personally conducted tour of the place. The little shops and the people were most interesting. Slim Chinamen, fat Chinamen, old solemn grandpas, and little plump boys who are pretty nearly Americanized, were all there in abundance. In the dirty little grocery shops which also seem to serve as restaurants, you could see men eating with chopsticks, or gulping soup out of a bowl. The food was almost all dried. There seemed to be almost nothing in the way of fresh fruit or meat, but everything was dried. There were dried duck, for instance, and lots of curious looking things that I couldnt tell whether they belonged to bird, fish, or flesh.

Then I came back to the Congregational Church, where they are holding their state Y convention, and heard John R. Mott make an adress at eleven o'clock. I was mighty glad to get a really closeup view of him. He certainly has a commanding personality. His talk was quiet, but very forceful. The central idea was the fact that in this day of action, and hurry, and activity, that it was more imperative than ever that we set aside an unhurried time, each day, for communion with God, in order to renew our spiritual strength, to develop our power of vision, to develop our power for helping others, and in order to give our spiritual lives a chance to appropriate and assimilate the good things that we receive all around us. There was one rather unusual sentence that he used that I think is pretty good. "Solitude is as necessary for the development of vision as society is for the development of character."

After his talk, he hurried away, but I got a chance to shake hands with him, and let him know that I was here. It seems that Porter is not in town, after all, but is expected today.

In the afternoon I took another sight seeing trip, this time through the Golden Gate Park, a beautiful park with all sorts of fine trees and flowers. I think that I liked the great big eucalyptus trees the best, with their fine green foliage and their bark shedding off in long strips. Then we drove over to the Cliff House and Seal Rocks. About this time it began to rain, so I was again prevented from taking any pictures. The seals looked like a bunch of brown muffs out on the rocks. At first they didnt move at all and I wasnt hardly sure that they were real seals, but finally one of them got up on his flippers and ambled to the edge of the rock and dove in. They are so clumsy looking that I dont see how in the world they manage to get up on the rocks which look very hard to climb. Then we drove over thru the Presidio, the great military base and fortification that guards the Golden Gate. Saw a lot of big guns, though they were not as big as the ones at Cape Cod or Fortress Monroe. We saw the Golden Gate from the most approved angle, too, but it wasnt so very impressive through the rain. We did, however, get some fine views of Frisco.

In the evening I went to the banquet of the state Y and met a bunch of U. of Cal. fellows and had a very good time. I heard Dr. Mott again and also saw Mr. Porter, who had just arrived. Dr. Motts talk was a very excellent interpretation of the place and the work of the Y as a whole. It was very well put, and very interesting.

Tuesday, Feb 21

The delegation to China, 1922. Top row, fourth from right: *Carl.* Fourth from left: *traveling companion Kenneth Latourette.* Seated, center: *delegation leader Dr. John Mott.*

The North American delegation to China: Top row, fourth from right: Carl, fourth from left: Professor Ken LaTourette, fifth from left: Professor Willis King, seated center: Dr. John R. Mott

After my last nights sleep on U.S. soil, I had breakfast, did a little late shopping, and was ready to go at a little after 10 oclock, so I took a taxi down to the pier and after locating my trunk, got aboard. It surely looked like a whopping big ship, and it was all decorated up with flags and pennants. The Japanese crew were bustling hither and yon, jibber-jabbering in great shape, and the two cranes, fore and aft, creaked and groaned and rattled as they loaded the supplies and baggage into the hold. I looked over the boat a little and then wrote a couple of letters and sent a telegram home. I couldn't find Porter or Case or any of the men that I knew, altho I knew that Case was aboard. I did run into Helen K. and Jean Kennedy and some of the other Y.W. girls and we went up on the promenade deck to wait until the boat pulled out. It is really exciting to watch a boat get ready to pull out. The last minute arrivals, rushing around worriedly, the crew bustling around, the people on the pier trying to carry on a shouted conversation with their friends on board, the hankerchiefs waving, the band playing, and then the big whistle toots three long toots, and we begin to move! Slowly we start with a little tug pulling us, and the people on shore wave their hats and shout and a group of Japanese students on the pier get together and give a funny college yell for somebody on board, and then we are really off. It was a slow trip thru the great bay, with one tug pulling us, and another at our stern, pulling it to one side or the other to steer the ship, and we had time to eat dinner and get out on deck before we were through the Golden Gate. I ate dinner with Mr. Porter and Prof. King, the negro prof. and after dinner I finally found Case, of whom more anon, as they say in the story books.

The trip through the harbor was great. First we passed five battle cruisers at anchor, then Alcatraz and Goat Island slipped by, the city of Frisco lay to the side and behind and then we went thru the Gate, with the sun making the white lighthouse almost glitter like snow.

Scarcely had we gotten out of the Gate, when it began to cloud up, and the wind began to pick up. Before land was out of sight, it looked real nasty and there were what landsmen would call waves, altho of course the old sailors said that it was still balmy. About this time I made the acquaintance of the whole Y and Y.W. delegation, so I will take time out to tell a little about each one.

Dr. Mott - tall, commanding, doesnt talk to anyone, and shows himself as little as possible.

Mr. Porter - Nat'l Student Secy. A very likeable middle aged fellow, a Rhodes scholar in his school days, and very easy to get acquainted with. I dont call him Dave yet, but I imagine that I may before we get back.

Prof. LaTourette - Very nice and not hardly at all professorial, as I had been told he was. I think that I will like him very much. He is only middle aged, a little older than Porter.

Prof. King - A fat, funny little negro, whom you might easily mistake for a Pullman porter, if you only looked at him. I want to get acquainted better with him. Prof. at Gammon Theological Sem.

Austin Case - A mighty nice fellow, not awfully aggressive, easy to get along with, from the Univ. of Washington.

Dr. Rutgers - head of the whole student movement of Holland. He talks "yust lak a Svede" and is a most hearty and enjoyable man. Inclined to be stout, and loves to talk.

Miss Katy Boyd George - Chairman of the Y.W. Committee on Friendly Relations with foreign students - a very handsome woman, rather small, with white hair, altho not white from old age, I don't think. Certainly she isn't much over 20 in spirit. She is one of the livliest of the party, and is the kind that simply impress you as "capable."

Miss Conrad - Dean of Women at Ohio State. - Tall, almost homely, but very nice.

Miss Sherman - Graduate of California - goodlooking - havent gotten acquainted as yet, because she hasnt been on deck.

Ruth Muskrat - 1/4 Indian blood. Looks rather like an Indian, too. Now I see why she has such an outlandish name. Dont know her yet. She was the first of the party to go under.

Jean Kennedy - Very goodlooking, and probably the youngest of the girls. Mount Holyoke girl. She seems to have brains as well as looks.

Mildred Tingley - from Purdue - a little older than the others, a darn good sport. She and I walked the deck all afternoon to keep our heads above deck.

Helen Kasbeer - Either she or Jean is the youngest girl. Helen is a good scout and stuck it out as long as any of the girls.

Lydia Johnson - U. of Minnesota. Rather slow Swedish type. Nice girl. (I hope that I havent forgotten anyone except Motts secretary, and one other Japanese that I dont know.)

Now to go on with the weather. It kept getting worse and worse. Mildred and I began to walk about 3 oclock. First we explored the whole blamed boat, even going up on the bridge until we were kicked off, as we knew we would be. We would stop a while and watch the waves or the gulls or the passengers until one or both of us began to feel kind of funny, and then we would start to walk again. Finally we found a swell place down on the main deck where the wind nearly knocked you off your feet, and the spray blew all over us, making our lips taste salty, and between wind and watching the spray blow, one would forget almost all about being sick. Finally, about 6:30 we were beginning to think about going in to get ready for dinner which comes at seven, but we thought we would wait until we saw one more big wave wallop us. The highest one previous had come within about four feet of the deck. Well, just as if Neptune was bringing us our order, a wave, the biggest I ever care to see, came a swooping up, and up, and up, and just naturally drowned us, and the deck and everything. You can see that it wasnt just spray, when I tell you that it went so high as to soak the next deck above, 10 feet higher. If we hadnt been standing behind a portion of rail that was solid we would have been ruined, but luckily we had been standing behind a solid rail four feet high, and that kept off the worst of it. It was plenty bad enough as it was. That wave simply fixed me. I wasn't even "woozy" after that, altho you could hardly walk the deck without staggering all over as if you were drunk. I went in then and got ready for supper. Mildred was going to eat supper, too, when I left her, but she lost her courage and didnt show up. Lydia and I were the only ones that showed up at our table of eight, and there were lots of tables that were entirely empty. Prof. LaTourette, who has crossed the Atlantic many times and has never missed a meal, came in and sat down at his table. He sat about two minutes, waiting for the waiter to bring his soup. Then he got up and left, looking pale as a ghost. Case had gone to bed early in the afternoon, and altogether the casualty list was large. I didnt eat a great deal for supper, but I felt one hundred percent better after I had eaten something, and went in and unpacked some of the things in my trunk and sat around and talked to Case to try and cheer him up. I wont brag, because one can never tell when it will get him, but I did feel pretty proud that I stuck it out, and even ate supper, when not more than 10% of the passengers were at supper. This old boat surely can roll, even though it is large. The experienced travelers say that they think that the cargo must be small, and that leaves her a bit top heavy. It was rough enough so that they had to put up the railings on the tables, and our plates would go scooting off across the table every time an extra good one struck us. It was great sport, and I wouldn't have missed it for anything. I went to bed and slept like a log, "rocked in the cradle of the deep."

Wed, Feb 22

On looking over what I wrote for yesterday, I find that it is abominably written, and very long. Today is going to be much shorter, even if written as badly. It was much calmer when we woke up, and the showing at breakfast was pretty good, altho many were still among the missing. I spent the morning doing some typewriting and a few other things. The afternoon was very profitably spent, I think. I simply set out to capture and hold up several of the people of the party, and rob them of their hidden treasure. I not only was very successful, but I opened up several real gold mines, which I will certainly follow up. First I talked for a long while with Prof. King, the negro. He surely is a white man under his coal black skin. We talked on all kinds of subjects, and I think that he had as good a time drawing me out, as I did getting him to open up. It seems to me that his mind and psychology, his "complex," so to speak, is typically that of a white man and not that of a negro, altho he has some of that strong emotionalism that we usually associate with the negro makeup. Then I had a most delightful talk with Prof. LaTourette, or "Ken," as I am beginning to call him. He is a most interesting man. He started out as a missionary to China, but after two years his health broke, and he has never been able to get back. He now professor of Missions at Yale Divinity school and has written several books about China and Japan. He is planning to stay over in China just about the same length of time as I am, except that he is planning to come back a little bit earlier, and as we began comparing notes on the places we wanted to see, I soon saw that it would be possible to go together if he wanted to do that. I didnt quite dare to suggest it though, because of course it wasnt my place to do that, but then he surprised me by suggesting it himself. If we can work it out to go thru China together, it will undoubtably be the most wonderful thing that could happen to me, because seeing China with him will be like seeing it twice, for he is a real authority on the subject, and could point out things and get into places that I couldnt possibly do. I surely hope that nothing interferes with that part of our scheme.

Then I had a fine talk with Miss George and Mrs. Mott, who was recuperating from a pretty severe attack of seasickness. I cant get enough of these talks with people who are really thinking people and who have such wide and varied experiences behind them.

It being Washingtons birthday, the dining room was all sported up fit to kill, and we had a swell seven course dinner that was without question the finest meal we have had on the boat. We sure have a good time at our meals because we are all so informal and just out to have the time of our lives. It was worth a nickel to see Porter and I each trying to get on the inside of a crab salad. Neither of us knew how to get thru the blooming beast's armour plate, for it was very poorly cracked. We made various rather startling efforts, and Porter chased a part of his crab into his lap. I didnt do quite so badly, but everyone had a good time trying to give us advice. We have a good table. Porter, King, Case, Miss Sherman, Lydia, Mildred, and myself. Prof. LaTourette has another table and Dr. Mott the third. Only high mucky-mucks sit at Motts table. I wondered as we were having our good times if Helen was having as good a time on her spree. After dinner some of us talked and talked, until 11 oclock and then went to bed.

Thursday, Feb 23

Woke up at six this morning and got up at seven. Went out and walked on deck for quite a while. My legs were actually stiff from walking so much with LaTourette and King yesterday. I typewrote a long letter home after breakfast and then walked and read until lunch. Shortly after lunch we had the first meeting of the whole delegation. Mott presided. The more I see of that man the more I admire him and the better I like him. He surely is a fine executive. In the delegation meeting we simply talked over things in general and decided to have a regular delegation meeting each day at three oclock.

    I surely love this ocean life so far. I have never had a better time in my life, and the congenial big family that we are multiplies the pleasure many fold. It is a lazy life if you want to make it so, but I am trying to make good use of my time, and at the same time, take life easy enough so that I will be in tip-top shape when we get there. I think that tomorrow I will describe a typical day on board, more in detail, but I think that I have done enough typewriting for today (about 7 pages) so I will quit.

Friday, Feb 24

True to my promise, I will try and depict our life here on this "floating palace of the deep." I generally rise a little before seven, and one can have toast and coffee in bed at that hour if he desires. Then I go up on deck and walk and read and talk with whoever is up at that early hour. Finally after a hungry hour in the fresh sea air, the breakfast bugle blows, and at 8:30 we all troop in and eat a substantial meal, more like dinner than breakfast. The waiters are all of them typical Japanese "boys," and it is awfully funny trying to get them to understand what we want. The only serious difficulty is encountered when someone orders one thing and then changes his mind and orders something else. The waiter always then brings <u>both</u> of the things you have ordered or else something entirely different. It is a lot of fun watching their faces as they try so hard to "savvy" what you are trying to say.

After breakfast I generally read or typewrite or walk or play quoits or something to while away time in the most useful manner possible. This morning I read 130 pages of a book on China before 11 oclock. At 11 oclock Togo or Kato or one of the other boys bring beef broth and crackers around the deck and we all partake. Then there is another two hour spell in which I usually try and get some exercise. At one oclock we have "tiffin" which is in plain English, lunch. After lunch is always a drowsy time until three oclock when we have our delegation meeting which will usually last until tea time at four oclock, when we have tea and cookies. Then from five to seven I generally walk the deck nearly all the time, talking with some one. At seven we have dinner, and we talk so long and eat so much that we are hardly ever thru before half past eight. Then the evening passes faster than any other period and we are usually ready to sleep. It is, of course, a very lazy life, but more fun than a box of monkeys and all of us have enough to do getting ready for the conference so that we are keeping our brains from atrophying.

Last night we had movies in the dining room at 8:30. They were quite some movies, but we had a good time making brilliant comments on them. The weather is getting very warm, so warm, indeed, that it is almost uncomfortable. There is still a fair wind blowing, tho, and it was cloudy and rainy earlier in the morning, tho it has cleared off by now, and the sun is very hot.

Saturday, Feb 25

I spent a little more than an hour up on the deck before breakfast reading and thinking. It was simply a beautiful morning, and I was way up on the tip top deck all alone. It surely is great up there in the early morning when it so nice and cool, and sky and air and sunshine all seem so fresh.

At breakfast Nakagawa, our waiter, informed us that the Siberia Maru was in sight and would soon be meeting us. Sure enough, right after breakfast, she hove, or possilby heaved, in sight, and passed us within a few hundred feet. Everybody was up on deck to see her go past. She was the first boat we have sighted since we have left Frisco.

At breakfast we decided to get up a funny little paper for our delegation. I was chosen editor in chief, with Mildred as associate editor. We chose the name suggested by Mr. Porter, "THE AUGUR, Warranted not to bore." We had more fun than a box of monkeys getting it up, and it made a great hit. Lydia was also one of the main conspirators and inspirators. The picture of Dr. Mott's eyebrows that Lydia drew made a great hit with the old boy. He chuckled and laughed all the while he was reading the thing, and Miss George tells me that he thought it was great.

In our afternoon delegation meeting Dr. Mott talked to us about the deputations that we will be sent on, and gave use a general idea of the type of message that we ought to offer. It simply appals me when I learn what they are going to expect of us. Have I a faith that is worth trying to impart to the Chinese students? That is the question that all of us undergraduates are simply challenged with. It is a testing time for all of us, and we are going to search our own lives and our own faith as we never have before. We have had many discussions already on lots of the doubtful points and I am thankful beyond words that we are with a group of leaders who are all forward-looking, young minded people, who are still building up their own faiths, not dogmatists who are sure that their own interpretation is the only hope. The more we talk and think, the more I am finding it possible to define what I myself believe, and what I consider non-essential. There may not be much to my creed as I would put it forth now, but I am at least pretty firmly convinced of a few things. I am sure that there is a God, who is a loving father. I am sure that Jesus Christ is my leader and Lord, and that I want to follow his principles of brotherhood. I am sure that his kingdom, as he called it, offers the only solution for the problems of the world. I dont think I am sure of much more than that, but I am sure of that, and I hope that in time my faith will grow, both in depth and breadth.

Sunday, Feb 26

I have just come from my first church service on board ship. An Episcopal minister led the service and Dr. Mott spoke. As usual, he was very good, and spoke on what seems to be his main message for at least the few times that I have heard him, namely that our spiritual life is the result of exercise, just as the development of our physical and intellectual life is the result of exercise. He can surely put that message and his plea for an exercise of our spiritual faculties in varied and powerful ways.

This morning at breakfast we got started on a discussion of whether a man had to believe in the deity of Christ to be a Christian, and that led to "What is a Christian?" and we sat at table thrashing things out and trying to thrash them out until ten oclock. That is the beauty of this life on ship-board, that when we get into a profitable discussion, none of us have to quit, so that we keep on until we either are worn out or else have arrived somewhere. We surely had a dandy confab this morning. I might explain here that we are not all at one table. Porter, King, Case, Stockwell, (Motts secy) and myself are the men, and Lydia, Mildred and Miss Sherman are the women at our table. Mildred and I about agree on most of these questions of religion, and we are uncertain on about the same points, so that we generally are the questioners and doubting Thomases in these discussions.

Tomorrow we get into Honolulu, and I will have to spend the rest of the day writing letters. I have letters for nine people already but am not nearly thru the list, so I've got to get busy.

Monday, Feb 27

This morning I woke at 6:30 as is my custom, and as also my custom, stood up in my berth and stuck my head out of the porthole to get a few whiffs of the cool fresh morning air. I was looking down at the waves, and then looked up a little and saw a queer looking cloud on the horizon. I sort of rubbed my eyes and then I began to realize that it was <u>land</u> off there in the distance! I dont think that anyone can realize the thrill that comes from sighting land unless he has done it for himself. The land was the first island of the Hawaiian group, of which we passed several in the course of the forenoon. They were very beautiful, in the fog and clouds, dimly visibel looming up out of the sea. Most of them were extinct volcanoes and often you could see the old crater basin, or rather the rim of it. Part of the morning I wrote letters, but I had finished most of the seventeen the evening before, so that I spent the greater part of the time up on deck, watching the sights. About 11 oclock we came in sight of Oahu, the island that Honolulu is located upon. It was a very pretty island and as we drew closer we could see thru my field glasses the coconut palms with their handfuls of foliage thrust high into the air. Soon we rounded Diamond Head, and came in sight of Honolulu itself. Diamond Head is a high old crater basin which juts out into the sea, about six or seven miles from the city. The crater was once full of active fire but now it contains only potential fire in the shape of great guns guarding the harbor. Down on the other side of the city, in Pearl Harbor, we could see two cruisers and eight submarines at anchor. The subs were wicked looking beasts. The sea was calmer than at any time since we have left Frisco, and the water was as clear and blue as saphire. A little launch came alongside bringing the pilot and the water was so clear that we could see the propeller as plain as anything. We were not brought to dock until 12:30 so that we had time to eat lunch on board.

As soon as we got off, we were met by cars from the Y.M., and the girls by people from the Y.W. We went out to the university of Hawaii first where Mr. Porter was speaking. (He and Dr. Mott had been brot in ahead of us by a tug, having been met out in the harbor.) The university is a nice little place, with about 300 students, of all races and mixtures of races, living together in the most perfect harmony. Chinese, Japanese, Hawaiian, Filipino, American, English, etc, and crosses between nearly all of them, are accepted on the same footing in the schools, and are all Americans. The Y. secretary there, Dwight Rugh, is nephew of the Arthur Rugh that I know, and is a peach of a fellow. He is only one year out of college, and is making a go of the work in an awfully hard field.

After we were thru at the U, we were driven up to see the Pali, (pronounced polly) a very high cliff where there is a wonderful view of about half of the island and the sea. While we were driving up there it started to rain, and by the time we got there it was <u>pouring</u>, and we couldnt see a single thing. We decided to wait just a few minutes and see if it wouldnt clear up a little. Sure enough after five minutes, the rain stopped, the clouds lifted, and there spread before us a most beautiful panorama, eighteen hundred feet below. The cliff is almost absolutely perpendicular, and the view is surely worth while. Coming back we passed thru Moana valley and watched the little waterfalls from the great cliffs on both sides. They were all small, but all larger than usual because of the hard shower. The highest one was a waterfall of fourteen hundred feet, just a beautiful, sparkling silver thread plunging down the rock. The drive both up and back was fine. The vegetation was typically tropical. There were acres of pineapples, and a great many small banana orchards. The trees were great. Tall, stately royal palms, with their white trunks, slender coconut palms, the widespreading monkey trees, and the great Chinese banyan trees I liked especially. The flowers were simply beautiful. Hybiscus shrubs, with their great delicate blossoms, were every where, and some of the lawns were just a riot of color.

It was very warm, even without a vest on. They say that the temperature doesnt vary more than a few degrees all year round, but remains about 70 - 85 at all seasons. It would surely be a wonderful place to spend a vacation. The shortness of our stay in Honolulu, (the boat left at six) made it impossible to get out to Waikiki Beach, but there was no surf riding to speak of, because the sea was too smooth, so that we didnt miss so much. It seemed good to get our feet on land again at first, but when we got back on again in the evening, it seemed mighty good to feel the roll of the old ship again. I sure love this life on the sea better than I had ever dreamed I would.

We came back on board rather loaded with spoils. We had mangos, the funniest tasting and juciest things I ever had in my mouth, and a big papaya, a sort of a melon thing that is a little better tasting than the mangos. Also the boat had gotten some strawberries and some _real_ cream, the first we have had of either, and I sure lit into them, getting away with two dishes of strawberries and cream, a piece of a mango, two slices of ripe pineapple (U-m-m!) and a little cake as my dessert.

Sunday, Mar 5

I had no idea that it had been so long that I had neglected to write in this journal. It has been a rather uneventful period since I last wrote, however, so that I havent omitted much. It is getting cooler as we draw awy from Honolulu towards the north. It seems good to be getting away from the heat. I suppose that they are having snow at home, but it has been about 70 or more every day with us.

There was one catastrophe this week. We lost a day somewhere in the mid Pacific, and havent been able to find it, tho nearly every one thinks that we will be able to pick it up when we come back. We went to bed on Thursday night and woke up on Saturday morning, Friday having been the unfortunate one to be lost. For the life of me, I cant get this time business straightened out. We have been setting our watches back about half an hour each day, depending on how far we went in that day. Then we go and drop out a day, which seems to me to be cancelling the effect of setting our watches back. It is too deep and complicated for me.

Just a day or so out of Honolulu we saw a school of porpoises, leaping out of the water and seeming to be having a great time. I had never seen them before. Then two days ago I saw eight or ten flying fish. They are small fish, not much over a foot long, I should say, and they fly for very long distances, a hundred yards or more. They have cute little wings.

Wednesday night we had a costume ball on board ship. Altho all of the delegation decided at first not to dance while on ship, some of the girls dressed up just for the fun of it, since you were supposed to come to dinner in costume also. Ruth Muskrat dressed up as an Indian, and she surely made a stunning looking Indian, much better looking than she is as a paleface. We had all sorts of fun all evening. First she did a war dance on deck which was very good, while I beat a tray borrowed from the deck steward to take the place of tom-toms. Then we just cut up generally, and taught the boat what a war whoop was like.

All this week we have been having some great old discussions on all sorts of questions, mostly on religious lines. We are literally hammering out our faith in the forge of discussion. It surely is great.

Last night it was very rough, even rougher than the first night, tho I didnt think that the boat rolled so much. The waves were simply great, and I went down on the stern of the boat, (that being the only place on the main deck that wasnt being washed by the waves every few minutes) and watched the old warhorses of the sea come smashing up at us, foaming at the mouth, and bound that they would crush us. The ship would always fool them tho by rising up over them, instead of being hit broadside. The beams and rivets groan and creak at the strain that is put upon them, and the noises make a delightful melody to put one to sleep.

It doesnt seem possible that in five days we will be in Yokohama. The voyage hasnt been long at all, and I really wish that we had about one extra week on board, because then I think that I would almost be ready to arrive and feel ready to do what is going to be expected of us.

I wonder what the folks are doing this nice sunshiny Sunday. I wouldnt mind being in the neighborhood of Chicago now.

Wednesday, Mar 8, 1922

This is another cloudy, rainy, morning without much news to report for the two days previous. Monday was the day decided upon by the editors for the publication of another Augur, so I had to give up several hours to that. It came off the press late in the evening and was distributed Tuesday A.M. at breakfast. I dont know whether it was because we called him a bushy-eyed sin-busting gent or not, but anyway Dr. Mott confided to Miss George that this group of students was the best behaved and the most sensible group he had ever traveled with. He said that we were full of life, and liked that, but we also knew how to conduct ourselves. He said that some of the members of the Japanese delegation which is on board had spoken to him about what a fine party we had. So we seem to be making an impression already.

Yesterday I had a long talk with Miss George about everything from theology to the question of whether we ought to be pacifists or not. Then Mr. Mitani, a splendid young Japanese who is third secretary for the Jpanese delegation to the League of Nations and who is now returning from the Washington Conference, came along and we all three talked about the problem of war. I had had a long talk with Mitani Sunday, so that we all were very frank in saying what we believed. He went so far as to say that he certainly was a pacifist in principle, though he could not say positively that if Japan went to war, he would refuse to answer the summons. He is a fine young Christian, not more than 26, I dont think, and with his mind, he ought to get to the top in the diplomatic circles some day unless I miss my guess. He has told me all sorts of interesting things about the League of Nations. He regards it as a failure in the same sense that the Articles of Confederation were a failure in our own country. That is, it is in itself a failure, but it has accustomed the people of the world to thinking of a world organization, and is preparing the way for such an organization.

I can not realize that in two more days we will be in Japan. Japan! Why if some one had told me three months ago that I would be in Japan before 90 days were up, I would have thot them a fit subject for the nut-house. Life surely is a mysterious and unsearchable pathway, and we need a faith and a trust that can believe in a guiding Hand.

This has been a short three weeks away from home, and I haven't had a single moment when I have even had a suspicion of homesickness. I have come nearer to being seasick than homesick.

Sunday, Mar 12, 1922

Here it is already Sunday, and no entry since last Wed. These days in the Orient have been so packed with new impressions and new sights that I have not taken time to write it up as I ought.

We had a rainy landing Friday afternoon, and of course were unable to see Fuji as we steamed into the harbor. Just before we got into dock, Admiral Togo, the hero of the great naval battle of the Russo-Japanese War, came on board to see Baron Kato, and the rest of the Japanese delegation to the Washington Conference. Admiral Togo looked like a tough old fellow, but one would have hardly picked him for the great man, any more than one would pick Baron Kato, tho the Baron somewhat looks the part. When we landed, we had to wait in the great warehouse where they unload the baggage, to claim ours, so we had a fine chance to watch the people and get a few first impressions. The police were guarding the place very carefully, and the situation was quite tense, as we could see when a gang of people tried to shove thru the police cordon and get into the place. It seems that the first member of the delegation to come back was greeted by rioting and the police were making strong efforts to prevent a repetition.

    I will admit that I couldnt feel the thrill of landing in Japan at first. Of course there were lots of Japanese but I had become accustomed to Japanese on the boat. There were pretty Japanese women, but I had seen them in Honolulu also. There were grizzled old coolies unloading baggage, but on the whole, they didnt look so different from the same class of workers in the States. It was not until, with the aid of Mr. Phelps and Mr. Jorgenson, who had met us at the dock, we had gotten our baggage thru customs without opening it, that I got my thrill at really being in Japan. We had sent the girls on ahead to their hotel and by the time that we had our baggage all fixed up it was six oclock, it was pouring rain, and we were all hungry as bears, having carried our trunks off the boat ourselves, because it was almost impossible even for Jorgenson to get a coolie. We stepped into the rain and called for rikshas. Jorgy jabbered something at them, we climbed in and started off. Each riksha had a little Japanese lantern hanging on the side so that we could see our riksha men quite plainly. It is a queer feeling to ride behind a human draft animal. It is something that I am afraid I would never get used to. As I watched my mans shoulders and hips swaying rhythmically under his short rubber coat, and his great broad rain hat, shaped like an inverted chopping bowl, bobbed up and down between the shafts, I couldnt help but think of the fact that he was a man, not an animal, and that he had a home, no doubt, and possibly a family, and - well, I dont know that I can describe it, but the idea of having a man lower himself to the position of draft animal in order to pull you around, is not pleasant. We ate supper at a fair restaurant, and then took the electric train to Tokyo, where we put up at the Seiyoken Hotel, after another riksha ride. I wish that I could adequately picture the thrill of those two short riksha rides. The curious little rikshas, the bobbing lanterns, the muddy streets, with no sidewalks, and with all sorts of traffic competing for the road, the queer little shops along the street, dimly seen thru the rain, and all the other picturesque sounds, sights and smells (I say that advisedly) made me realize for the first time, the fact that I was really in the Orient.

Saturday we got a rather late start on the day, partly due to the fact that Mr. Porter had to be put back to bed with the flu, his cold of the day before having developed into a mild case of the flu. After he was tended to Mr. Patterson of the Y took the rest of us men around the city in cars. We went out to Shiba Park, Uyeno Park, and out thru the buildings of the Imperial University before lunch, but tho those things were interesting, they were not half as interesting to me as simply the common sights that we saw along the way. The streets and the traffic is more interesting to me as yet than any Shoguns shrine. The first thing that impresses one about the street traffic is the fact that almost everything is done by man power. It is simply amazing to one from the West. All the hauling is done either by men hauling great carts loaded to the limit, or by poor little horses, which are always lead, never driven by their coolies. These coolies are of many types, and all of them very interesting, I am sure if one only knew the story back of their usually stolid faces. Some of them are old grizzled veterans, very close cousins, I am afraid, to the poor little horses with whom they are competing. Some of them are young men, with splendid physiques, and great broad chests, who dont seem to be taking the work as a harship at all. Some of them are little boys, no more than 14 or 15, hauling small carts with big loads, and still with some spirit left. They haven't yet been broken into good draft animals, but no doubt will be. There is also some competition for the coolies in the form of oxen, also small, to fit the size of the country, but the horses and oxen havent much chance against the human animal, for the human animal is willing to work for less, and thus beat out the horse and ox in the struggle for existence. But to get away from the sociological aspect and back to the pictorial. Aside from the patient coolies drawing their loads of all sorts and descriptions there are school children, dressed in uniform, playing and laughing, little girls in flowery colored kimonos, sometimes carrying on their backs babies almost as big as they are, and then everywhere there are the dainty little Japanese women. If there is one thing I like especially about Japan, it is the Japanese women. In their neat, dainty dresses, with their broad multicolored sashes, tied in a great bow at their backs, their white stockinged feet thrust into their clickety-clackety clogs, they surely make a picture. From the top of their carefully dressed hair to the sole of their little clogs, they seem to typify all that we like to think about Japan. And now that I have gotten around to Japanese women, I will stop my description and take you to the splendid Japanese luncheon that we had, served by these aforementioned, shuffling little ladies. We went to a Japanese restaurant, where we met Jorgy, and several fine Japanese, among whom was Mr. Saito, the head of all Y work in Japan, even over Phelps and Jorgy, who are absolutely willing to work for him. Saito is certainly a fine-looking man, and I wished that I had sat where I could talk with him. But to get to the meal. We took off our shoes on entering the place and went upstairs to a private room. We sat crosslegged before the little low table, which had a small gas burner every few feet. Two of us sat at each burner, one oneach side of the table, which was only about 15 inches wide. They brot in a small copper dish, rather shallow, which we set on the burner, and then they gave us the material for a Japanese guenabi luncheon. First they pour in some bean oil sauce, called shoyu, then a sort of vermicelli, several slices of bean curd are laid in the dish, a few sliced onions are scattered over the concoction, and some thinly sliced beef is laid on top. When it has boiled and stewed for about ten mintues, and the smell nearly drives you frantic with hunger, you take a bowl of rice and put some of the guenabi on it and eat it all with chopsticks. I dont think I have eaten as much for a long time as I ate at that meal. It surely was good, and we got away with an awful pile of it. That one dish is the whole meal. There is no entree, and no dessert, so one is obliged to eat a lot to fill up on.

After lunch it was about two-thirty, so we immediately went out to the home of Mr. Asano, the head of the T.K.K. Line, who had invited all the first class passengers of the Taiyo Maru out to his home for tea. It was a beautiful place, very splendid and rich as would be expected, but hardly a typical Japanese home. We had a very nice time and they also had an interesting entertainment for us.

Sunday, March 12

We went to church this morning at a Japanese church, the largest in Tokyo. Of course we couldnt understand a word that was said, but it was very interesting nevertheless. Dr. Wemura, the minister, seemed like a very able man. The audience was made up of high class people, for the most part, full as high class as the average American church. It was a special service for Parliament and the govt, and the opening and closing prayers were offered by members of Parliament who are members of the church. The church building and interior looked for all the

Initial impressions of Japan: Sightseeing a Tokyo canal

world like a small town church in America. The uncomfortable pews, the wheezy organ, were all there. The thing I wonder at, after seeing some of these temples and shrines, is that the people will leave such beautiful buildings to worship in a shabby looking Christian church. It speaks well, alright, for the real vital content of our religion.

    We had lunch at the Phelps, where all the members of the Y staff, and some missionaries were invited, as well as all the men of the Peking delegation. There were about thirty there and we had a dandy luncheon, served cafeteria style. Mrs. Phelps and Mrs. Jorgenson are both very fine women, I thot.

    In the afternoon we went to the Unoin church for foreigners to hear Dr. Mott speak. He gave one of the best and most statesmanlike addresses I have ever heard him make. His main thot was to dispel the pessimism which he feels is prevalent among many Christian people. He summed up very well the causes for such pessimism and then went ahead to show why he thot that the present was one of the great days for the church, providing she saw and made the most of her innumerable opportunities.

Monday, March 13

This has been a memorable day. Case and I decided last evening to go with the ladies of the party up to Nikko, since the rest of the men were busy in one way or another. Porter is still in bed, but feeling somewhat better.

We met Miss George and the rest of them at the Imperial Hotel at quarter to eight, and after some wild excitement about getting taxis managed to catch the 8:30 train to Nikko. The scenery going up there was certainly picturesque. We passed thru some very fine farming country, and it was fascinating to see tiny farms and people at work in the fields, and all the strange sights. The farmers' houses are, as a rule clustered together in small hamlets, and the fields ar all outside the village. The houses are tiny, and instead of the tile roofs of the city, one sees nothing but thatched roofs. Most of the houses are quite neat and clean in appearance, tho of course there are exceptions. One is impressed by the scarcity of animals even in the country. One can pass through miles of rice paddies and tiny wheat fields, and see only one or two scraggly little ponies, and no cattle, nor even any dogs or cats. Food is too precious to feed it to animals. Every inch of ground is cultivated. The wheat is grown in rows, and hoed by hand. Most of the ground is carefully terraced so as to make each field level, and prevent loss from washing. The steep hills are all planted to forest trees, so as to provide the future generations with fuel and lumber. The bamboo seems to grow everywhere, and makes a very pretty green growth. It did not seem at all like winter, with the winter wheat all green, and all the pines and bamboo growing so luxuriantly.

After several hours traveling thru these little toy rice paddies, each one separated from the next by a low mud wall, we began to come in sight of the mountains. It is curious to think of mountain in Japan. Somehow we never think of Japan as being mountainous, but the mountains we began to see were certainly not toy mountains. About this time, too, we first saw the mulberry bushes, each bush carefully tied up for winter. We crossed many little mountain brooks, and every now and then we would see an old water wheel, turning leisurely beside a little thatched hut, with usually three or four dirty little urchins, in kimonos that had once been brightly colored, playing around near the water, but showing no signs of having come in contact with it.

As we climbed up and up, we soon came in sight of the famous avenue of cryptomerias which leads into Nikko. These cryptomerias are wonderful old trees, great tall, stately fellows, planted about three hundred years ago by one of the shoguns whose father is buried at Nikko. They are now from one hundred to one hundred and fifty feet high, and the long avenue lined on both sides with these old shoguns of the forest, makes one of the most magnificent sights I have ever seen.

Almost as soon as we got to Nikko, we went out to see the Shinto shrines there. They form a large group of buildings halfway up the side of a large hill, and are situated in an immense grove of cryptomerias. The shrines themselves are beautiful beyond description, and ornamented to a degree that is almost beyond belief. Every cranny, no matter how obscure, is carved, and lacquered and inlaid with brass, as if it was the most prominent part of the temple. The buildings are all lacquered with a fine red lacquer, and the ornaments and carvings and decorations under the eaves are colored blue or

"The shrines themselves are beautiful beyond description."

yellow or white, and the color scheme is most striking. To me tho, the most remarkable thing about them all was the amount of detail work and the care with which it had been done. There seems to have been no end to their patience and careful workmanship.

We went into the main shrine, and the decoration inside even surpassed that on the outside. Whole panels of the wall were carved out of one piece of wood, the carving being of the most intricate nature. The ceiling was most beautifully lacquered with pictures and designs. The shrines have a spirit of reverence and worship about them that it is impossible to deny. There are no images in Shinto shrines, and the sole object that the people look up to during their worship is a round metal mirror hanging on the wall. The mirror is, as I understand it, supposed to represent the idea of truth, and also the idea of finding ones god in ones self.

When we had looked thru the shrines, far too hastily to suit me, we took cars and went out into the mountains, past some copper mines, and the cars finally stopped at a little cluster of houses, where we got out and walked for about half an hour, up a most magnificent mountain gorge, to the Hoto waterfalls. The falls were fine, but the walk up the canyon was worth the walk, even if we hadnt seen the falls. The ladies of the party, especially Miss George, were pretty near all in when we finally reached the top and came in sight of the falls. We had tea up on the summit there, and then came back. Unfortunately, it started to rain a little, so I was not able to get any pictures of the canyon. I have had tough luck all along with the sun. I think I had better make some kind of an offering to appease his anger.

We had dinner at the hotel and then took the train back, arriving at Tokyo a little before eleven. They have a saying here that one cannot say the word magnificent until one has seen Nikko. I heartily agree.

Tues, Mar 14

Today was rather a prosaic day. We slept rather late to make up for the hard day previous, and then went to the bank, then to the Tourist bureau to get our railroad tickets, and by that time it was lunch time, and we went to another Japanese restaurant and had another gunabi luncheon. I sure like them. Our guide for the morning was Mr. Yuasa, a student from the Imperial University here, who is one of the six undergraduate delegates going to the Conference from Japan. He is a very fine fellow, and speaks English quite well. It is impossible to appreciate the language barrier between ourselves and the Japanese. In almost any other country in the world one can at least make a guess at the meaning of signs, etc, but here they are as unintelligible as if they were in Sanskrit. The number of people that can speak English is not as great as one might imagine. It would be a fright trying to travel alone in the Orient if one did not know some one to whom to go for advice and information.

In the evening we went over to the Imperial Hotal (Case and I) and had supper with the girls.

Wednesday, Mar 15

New impressions! New impressions! Today has surely been full of them! We left Tokyo at 9:30 on a cute little train, with a nice observation car. Everything in this country is small, including the people, and the trains conform to the standard. I cant go thru a door in this train without bending my head, and the cars are so much narrower than ours at home, that it gives one the impression of being on a toy train, and we certainly are riding thru a country of toy farms and farmhouses, with little toy towns every few miles. The service and accomodations and speed on this line compare very favorably with the best on American lines, tho the roadbed leaves something to be desired, which accounts for the terrible typing of this sheet and the two previous.

We had supposed that this trip would be a rather uneventful and more or less prosaic trip thru farming country much like we saw on our way to Nikko, but it has surely exceeded all our expectations. I think that the biggest surprise of the whole trip has been the amount of mountainous country we have passed thru. Somehow I have never realized how rough Japan is. We began to get into low mountains almost as soon as we were out of Yokohama, and as we were looking at them, I peered ahead, and all of a sudden my breath kind of stopped, for there, there,

there, was Fuji! For four days we have been in Tokyo, and every day it has been hazy enough so that we couldnt see the white head of the famous old mountain of Japan. We had been very much afraid that it was going to be too cloudy today to see it, too, but luck was with us. All that I can say about it is that even after all the pictures we have seen of it, and all the paintings, Fuji itself was no disappointment. It was better than the best picture of it I have ever seen, and that is as far as I can go in trying to describe it. At first it was far in the distance, but we drew nearer and nearer to it, until we passed right by its foot. When we were far away, it kept its head unveiled, but when we came too near, it became shy, and hid its head behind a cloud that it snatched out of the clear blue sky. After we had passed it became still more veiled, until we could see little more than its base.

The country beyond Fuji was almost Swiss in its mountain scenery. We would whisk into a tunnel, out for a moment to cross a tumbling mountain stream, then back into the black heart of the mountain again. Every now and then we would come upon a large factory with a cluster of houses around it, located by the side of a stream, making good use of the abundance of water power. Thru the worst of the grade, we had one engine pulling and one engine pushing us. The rugged mountains and deep wooded gorges were just great, prettier, if anything, than the mountains that I saw in the west. Even in the mountains, every available bit of ground was cultivated, and that which could not be cultivated was planted to trees.

As we left the steepest of the mountains behind us, we came into the most prosperous farming country that we have seen yet. Wheat seemed to be the main crop, though the rice fields were very frequent, all of them about the size of a small garden plot. It is simply impossible to conceive of the labor that the people will go to, to make a bit more ground available; every field that is not level is terraced, to make it safe from the ravages of rain; the fields almost nibble at the roads in an attempt to steal a bit more of the precious soil; there are no fences, for they would take up room; there are no broad meadows, first because there are no animals to feed, and second because land is too valuable to be useful to grow grass; and I am not exaggerating when I say that the miles and miles of country that we have passed thru today are much more intensively cultivated than any experimental plots that I have ever seen at the university. There a few plots of wheat are grown in rows and hoed by hand; here it is done in no other way; there the paths between plots are made two feet, as being the minimum width possible; here one never sees fields separated by more than a six inch mud wall a few inches high, or at the most by a little footpath a couple of feet wide. The orchards are a marvel of painstaking care. The trees are all trimmed off perfectly level on top and a lattice of bamboo is made which spreads over the whole orchard at the same height as the tops of the trees. Then when the peaches, for instance, form, each peach is tied up and enclosed in a paper bag to protect it. I tell you we are getting an object lesson of the lengths to which people will go when the struggle for existence is keen. The houses look very neat and prosperous, and their mossy thatched roofs speak of stability and old age. Nearly every farmhouse and cluster of farmhouses is surrounded by a hedge or a row of trees, which I suppose help to supply fuel for cooking, for no fuel is used for heat, even in the best homes, unless it be a very little. Sure it is cold, but they get used to it.

  We have also passed many tea plantations, if anything as small as that can be called a plantation, and the tea makes a very interesting sight. It is a small bush, and grows low and rounded on top, so that rows of tea look like rows of hedges side by side.

This afternoon we have been within a few miles of the sea almost all the way, and every little while it surprises us by appearing on our left. The boats that the fishermen use are most curious, and look very clumsy to me. The sea has been just as blue as crystal, and has been a welcome sight. It almost makes me long for the old Taiyo.

Altogether it has been one of the most interesting days I have had since I have left home. It has been a continuous moving picture show all day long, except that it has been better than any movie, just as the real thing is always better than the best picture of it. I dont think that I can ever forget those terraced mountainsides, the flooded rice-paddies, the patient peasants with their primitive hoes, and their heavy two wheeled carts, and I am quite sure that I can never forget that grand old knig of mountains, Fujiyama.

Thursday, March 16

This morning we went over to a lacquer works after breakfast. First tho, I must tell about the splendid service we are getting at our hotel. They have the classiest little Japanese maids that I have ever seen, and they take care of us as if their lives depended on it. I must confess that they take better care of us than they do of the girls. A pretty little maid in a beautiful Japanese kimono, with a big obei tied around her waist and done up in a big bow on her back comes in at 7 and wakes us and makes our little coal fire in the fireplace. That is the only heat they have in the hotel, but the weather hasnt been cold at all, so the nice little fire has been enough to keep us warm, and I don't know of many nicer ways of being woken up than to have our little maid come in. The service at all of these Japanese hotels has been fine, but this one has got them all beaten a mile.

Well, as I started out to say, we went to the lacquer works first this morning and watched them making the most beautiful pieces of lacquer work you can imagine. Lacquer juice is the juice of a tree, and they mix it with various ingredients and dyes to make the lacquer they want. To make an extra good piece of lacquer work it is necessary to put on thirty or forty coats of lacquer, drying each coat thirty hours and then polishing it. They surely have patience and skill in doing the work.

Then we went to the damascene establishment, and watched them for a while. They take the steel, a steel plate for instance, and hammer into it tiny gold wires, to make the design they want. Then they heat it enough so that the gold is really fixed in the steel, and then polish and touch it up.

The cloissone shop, was, I think, the most interesting of the three, tho. It is quite a complicated process, rather too complicated to describe, but the principle is this. They take a copper vase, for instance, and build up on it with a very narrow copper ribbon, set on edge, the design they want. Then they fill in the places between the copper bands with different colored enamel, and bake it, enamel again and bake it, repeat the process again and again bake it, and then polish it down to a most beautiful finish. Most of the pieces they make are simply products of very fine workmanship, but they had some pieces that were real works of art, and that are surely tempting. If I were a millionaire, I am sure that I would spend a lot of money in that shop.

In between shops and in the afternoon we looked at temples. There are a great bunch of old temples here in Kyoto, all of them very impressive, tho none of them nearly as beautiful as the shrines at Nikko. At the Higashihonganji there was a long coil of rope about three inches thick which had been used in making the temple. What do you suppose it was made of? Well, they needed a very strong yet reasonably small rope to lift the immense timbers for the pillars, etc, so the women of Japan cut off their hair by the thousands to make this rope. It surely is an impressive memorial to the devotion of the people. At the Sanjusangendo they had a thousand images of Kwannon, the Goddess of Mercy. It is interesting that for the goddess of mercy they have a goddess with a hundred hands, signifying, I suppose, her power of helping people. At the Kiomidzu there are several very old and very impressive shrines and temples, situated on a beautiful old hill overlooking the city. The plum trees in the grounds were all in bloom, which certainly added to the beauty, and I can easily see that in cheery blossom time the whole city would be a regular fairyland.

Kyoto itself is a most delightful old city. For over a thousand years it was the capital of Japan, and as the imperial city was well built and well kept up. It is entirely surrounded by great hills, and it surely is an inspiring sight to wake up early in the morning and watch the sun gradually sweeping the blue mist from the tops of the hills out of your hotel window. One can't help but sort of absorb a sense of power from their splendid strength. The sights and sounds of the city are typically Oriental, and the people stare at us much more than they did in Tokyo. Poor Prof. King surely draws the crowds. You see they almost never see an African out here, tho they may now and then see a Hindu, and most of the people have probably never seen a black man, so that their curiosity is at least excusable. There are almost no foreign stores here, and the whole city is the product of Japan, very little mixed with English or American influences, except of course indirectly. In spite of its age, the city is the cleanest I have seen since leaving America, and all the people we have come in contact with, are the finest kind of examples of the real Japanese.

About five thirty we went out to the Imperial University and met some of the fine young students and the older student who is acting as student secretary for the university Y while carrying on his school work. They were a fine keen bunch and were very anxious to have me spend several days with them on my way back in July. It is very possible that I may, for it would be an ideal opportunity to get next to the Japanese students.

We went to bed fairly early in order to get an early start the next morning for Nara, the little beauty spot around here, about an hours ride out of Kyoto.

My Impressions of Japan

Kobe, Japan
March 19, 1922

Dear Mr. Wolfe:
In my last letter I told you about our interesting stay in Tokyo, and our trip down thru the mountains and rice paddies to Kyoto. I made an attempt to describe some of the impressive old temples and shrines that we saw, and tried to picture some of the Oriental street life of these Japanese cities. I think I will try in this letter to give you some of the general impressions that I have gained from this ten days trip thru Japan. You may think that ten days is too short a time to form any opinions, but when one fills the days as full as we have, it is possible to learn a good deal in even that short period.

MY TRIP TO CHINA

To begin with, I must say that the Japanese people have won my respect and admiration to a degree that I did not think possible. They are an extremely industrious people, as even the most casual observer must see. From their busy bustling crowds on the streets of Tokyo to the hardworking farmers out in their little toy wheat fields near Kyoto, everyone seems to have his work to do. There almost no beggars, fewer even than in American cities. The little shops are, in general, very neat and clean, and the tiny farms are models of the most painstaking care. Kobe and Osaka are great thriving industrial cities, with an array of black smokestacks comparable to that of many large American cities. Not only are the people industrious, but they are thrifty. I noticed their thrift particularly in the farming regions, where every morsel of ground is conserved with scrupulous care, and the neat little thatched houses were much more prosperous looking, and much cleaner than the cotton belt farmhouses of America.

These qualities of the Japanese I was more or less prepared for, but some of their finer characteristics were somewhat of a surprise, after what we have heard of Japanese militarism. For one thing, they are such a cheerful, good natured, people that it is impossible to keep from liking them. From the laborers and 'riksha men to the university students, I think they are much more cheerful, and at least one hundred per cent more courteous, than Americans. They seem to be very kind to their children, too, and the bright, pretty clothes they dress them in show the pride they take in their babies.

Another thing that strikes me particularly is their progressiveness. As I stood on the street corner of

Tokyo, waiting for a street car, it made me sort of gasp to realize that these motor cars and bicycles, tooting their way thru the crowds, and these big stone buildings, everything modern, in fact, has been introduced in the last seventy years. All that I can say is that it isnt safe to prophesy any limit to the future of this little island kingdom when we see the progress that it has made in the past two generations. It is a curious mixture of old and new, this country, and it is well typified, I think, by these school boys we see, dressed in kimonos and clumsy wooden clogs, just like their forefathers for generations back, but riding to a modern school on a modern bicycle made in Japan.

   As to the bugaboo of Japanese militarism, my attitude has certainly changed during the last ten days. A problem like that looks so differently when viewed from the inside! A days trip thru the farming country where every available inch of land is seized upon and cultivated, has been a mighty fine object lesson in the scarcity of land and the lack of room to expand. It is the most natural thing in the world that a party should grow up whose policy is agression and the acquisition of land. I dont want to excuse the militaristic policy, but I simply want to point out that there are some mighty strong economic reasons for such a policy. What chances I have had to talk with Japanese students, however, have been very reassuring, and a private conversation between Dr. Mott and Baron Kato was even more hopeful. I am convinced that the thinking people of Japan realize that they are only going to play a losing hand if they attempt a military expansion. The Washington Conference was a tremendous help in showing Japan that other countries, and especially the U.S., are dead in earnest in their desire to bring permanent peace. Japan learned her militarism from Europe, and she has proved a mighty good pupil. It looks now as though she were going to pattern her ideals after the ideals of the Washington Conference, and although the military party is still strong, I think that as a ruling factor in Japans policy, its end is in sight.

I expect you are greatly interested, too, in the progress that Christian workers are making here. My ten days in Japan have at least convinced me of this, that Buddhism and Shintoism as religions for the educated classes, are almost extinct. The ignorant classes still follow the well worn path, but the thinking people, whether they all admit it or not, are practically agnostic. Undoubtably there lies the great opportunity of Christianity - to step in and fill with a vital faith, the place which has been left by the old discarded forms.

As far as I have had opportunity to observe, the Christian work in the universities is very strong, though of course not as extensive as the work at home. Their strength lies, I think, in the fact that here they have no half way Christians. A man is either a pretty strong Christian or he is not a Christian at all. It is a sifted group to begin with. The students are certainly capable of carrying on the work themselves. At the Imperial University in Kyoto, they have a Y of 200 members in a university of 2000, and have no student secretary. The work is being carried on, however, by a fine young law student who has a cabinet of six fellows under him, and they seem to be putting on a fine piece of work. For instance, in their small Y dormitory, almost every one *of the twenty men in the building comes out each morning to a Morning Watch meeting before breakfast. These meetings are held the year around, and the meeting is conducted by a different student each morning. I don't think that our American associations can offer anything finer.*

I count it a real privilege to have known some of these keen young Japanese students. They are some of the finest Christian fellows I have ever known. I wish I could tell you more about some of them, but my time it getting short, and I've got to close. Give my regard to all the fellows. Best wishes for the Y work during this semester, and especially for the new officers when they are elected.

Sincerely,

Carl

Friday, March 17

This morning we went out to the Doshisha, the large Congregational school and college here in Kyoto. It is quite a large school, looking very much like a middle western academy in the States. We were shown around by an old Wisconsin man, Prof. Grover, of the class of '06, and the president, a Japanese who was a very fine old fellow. We also saw some of the girls and the buildings of Miss Florence Dentons school for girls, but we didnt have time to go in.

We took the 10:52 train for Nara, and had an hours ride thru very fine farming country. Nara is a rather sleepy little old town at the foot of some great old hills, and the temples are most of them located at the foot or part way up the mountains. Nara was the first permanent Japanese capital, and is a very old city. The temples and shrines are all located in a beautiful old park, Nara Park, where hundreds of sacred deer wander around thru the trees or come and eat biscuits out of your hand. They are pretty little deer, and tame as can be. Some of the temples are nearly a thousand years old and look somewhat like an old Indian blockhouse. They are entirely made of wood, and certainly look their age. They are the second oldest wooden buildings in Japan, and about as old as any wooden buildings anywhere in the world. There is also an old bronze bell, of tremendous size, that one rings with a steel-capped log suspended from the ceiling.

The winding paths thru the trees are all lined with old stone lanterns, of all shapes and designs, almost no two of them exactly alike, set up during all these centuries by people who wished to show their reverence for the place.

The most impressive thing at Nara, though, I thought, was the great Daibutsu Buddha. It is located in an immense temple, some 200 feet long and 160 feet high, all of wood, as usual, and built about 1600. The image itself is a great seated Buddha, much older than the temple, dating back to about 800, I believe, though is has had a rather a checkered history, and has been partially recast at times. It is of bronze, a dark green with age, and when one enters the temples, its 53 feet of bronze look more like a hundred and fifty. It is simply huge. With the placid, almost scornful look of the typical Buddha, it looks down on us as merely the fleeting creatures of the moment, while it belongs to the ages. In spite of its impressiveness, tho, it is very evident from the people that come, that as an object of worship it appeals only to the ignorant and uneducated classes. Buddhism as a religion for educated classes is dead.

In the evening we got back to Kyoto for supper with the girls at the home of Mr. Grafton, the Y secretary.

Saturday, March 18

We left Kyoto at 8:45 and rode down to Kobe, where I bought my steamer ticket home on the Empress of Asia, leaving Yokohama July 22. Kobe is a very uninteresting city as compared to Kyoto. It is a very foreign city, and the streets are almost as much English and American in places as they are Japanese. The hotel we stayed at is down in the old foreign concession, also, so that it was a very English atmosphere. There is no foreign concession now, of course, but it was not so long ago when this part of the city was entirely under the rule of foreign governments, each government having its own little piece where it tried all criminal cases, and had complete jurisdiction. The Japanese had no say whatsoever. These concessions still exist in China, and it is going to be interesting to see them. Kobe is very much of an industrial city, and of course with the bringing in of the American industrial system, comes the American greed for money, and the exploitation of the people. I wonder if Japan will have to go thru the long fight for the reasonable rights of labor that America has had to go thru. Some of the soums that we walked thru Saturday certainly look as if she had a good start in the same direction.

This question of industrializing Japan is a most puzzling and complex one. It seems quite evident that Japans only hope lies in being industrialized, because she can find no new unsettled land in which to expand. The white races have grabbed every available colonizing site, and the only solution for Japan is to increase the number of industrial establishments in order to employ her ever growing population. Yet when she does that, she immediately brings in all these other problems of industrialism that are almost as hard to solve as her original problem of expansion. Is Japanese labor going to have to go thru the same fights as American labor, or the even more terrible history of English labor, or will Japan profit by our experience and not attempt to exploit its labor. If Japanese labor should be so exploited that it attempted revolt, then look out for some real Bolshevism. It has been very interesting to me that to find that we have a few Christian workers who seem to be in very close touch with the leaders of the labor movement, and I hope that the labor movement can be so influenced that it will not become as materialistic as the American labor movement, for instance.

The industrial problems are not felt so keenly by most Japanese yet as they are in America, but with their growing industrial life, it will not be long before they will have to face them.

Sunday, March 19

Went to church this morning and heard a noted Quaker, Dr. H.T. Hodgkin, give a very fine sermon. He has a remarkably interesting message, but he is going to be one of the main leaders at Peking, so I wont try and enlarge on his idea now, but will wait until I know more about it. In the afternoon I busied myself writing letters, and in the evening we got into a long discussion inspired by Dr. Hodgkin, as to whether war was ever justifiable, and what the Christian attitude toward war should be. It was some discussion, and lasted until 12. As we were leaving town at 7:55 the next morning, it made a rather short night, as we had to get up at 6.

Monday, March 20

This has been one of the most beautiful days that we have had since we left home. The trip from Kobe down to the end of the island has been simply one grand panorama of changing scenes; rice paddies, mountains, hills, fishing villages, great broad rivers, and the beautiful inland sea.

There were many interesting things in the morning; the train was taking us rapidly into warmer country and it looked more and more like summer. For the first time we saw rice growing in the fields, and the men and more often the women out in the water up to their ankles, weeding the rows. The rice is a very slender wiry looking plant when it is small, and a darker green even than the winter wheat.

During the afternoon we rode for a long time within sight of the inland sea. The little thatched huts of the fishing villages were most interesting. They were the same general type as the farmers houses, one storied, with thin wooden walls, and a very neatly thatched roof, but they were not as prosperous looking as the farmhouses. In many places there were ponderous stone or earth dikes to keep the sea from rushing in on the little rice fields. The fishermen in many places have placed weirs, crude little bamboo traps, across the mouth of the rivers that empty into the sea, and catch the fish as they go up the river to spawn.

The scenery along the coast is the best I have seen anywhere since I have started. The mountains and jagged rocks formed a "stern and rockbound coast," and the rocky islands off the coast were about as fine as anything of that sort I have ever seen. In some places there were rocky reefs where the breakers were breaking and casting great clouds of spray into the air, for the wind was very strong.

The craft were as interesting as the sea itself. There were

many of the large, clumsy fisherman's dories being sculled along by means of the large orr at the stern; there were little native coasting boats, with patched old sails; and now and then we would see a larger freighter steaming along.

We got to Sheminoseki right on time (all Japanese trains seem to be right on time) and got our baggage transferred to the boat. We were all prepared for a rough night, for we knew how strong the wind was, but we were a little surprised to find that the passenger steamer that had set out for Fusan in the morning had had to give up and come back, because it was too rough to cross. However the officers of the boat thought we could make it all right, and they were going to make another try, anyway, so we steamed out of the long harbor. There was surely some gale blowing, but it didnt bother most of us. Austin, Mildred, Jean, and myself even went so far as to have some bread and jam and tea before we went to bed. I slept like a log, though every now and then when I woke up, the boat seemed to be doing its best to stand on its head. It didnt roll so badly, but it pitched and bucked as badly as I have ever wished to try it.

Tuesday, Mar 21

By the time we woke up in the morning the sea was very much smoother, and we were passing into the harbor of Fusan before we were through breakfast. It was a very imposing harbor, with fine high rocks on each side of the entrance. As usual, there were many quaint little boats with sails of all forms and designs, manned with a large crew of one, two, or three, men.

On the docks we saw our first glimpse of the Koreans. They are certainly a crude looking people. I think that they are the least civilized in appearance of any we have seen. The typical Korean costume is all white; white trousers, and white stockings with a long white robe over all. Then they wear on their heads these ridiculous little stove pipe hats, made of black wire gauze, and carry long pipes, sometimes as long as their arms. As it was a cold day, most of them had a skull cap under their stovepipe, or in some cases, a big fur cap, on top of which, at a precarious angle, was perched thier little black flea-catcher. Of course there were many variations of this costume worn by the coolies and dock men, and in most cases it required quite a stretch of the imagination to call their clothes white. They were a pretty tough looking lot, with their thin scraggly, chinwhiskers, which seem to be discouraged in early youth, from their puny growth. The Korean porters have a most curious wooden frame which they carry on their back to support the enormous loads that they carry. We saw many little boys, some of them certainly not more than 15, with these frames on their backs, waiting for a load to carry.

We only had time for a fifteen minute walk thru the main street of Fusan, and then we got on board the train, and started off for Seoul. It was a fascinating trip. We were passing all day through the mountains and hills of southern Korea, and thru the main farming section of the country also. The country seems much poorer than anything we saw in Japan, almost poverty-stricken, in fact. The houses are mud walled huts, or built of stones held together with clay, with low thatched roofs. The roofs simply cannot be compared with the thatched roofs of Japan, however. In Japan a thatched roof is at least a foot thick, and is a real work of art. In Korea a thatched roof is straw tied onto the roof poles. The dooryards are dirty and unkempt, in sad contrast to the neat little yards that we have been seeing.

The fields are much the same as in Japan, except that they are not as intensively cultivated, and the crops are not as far along, because it quite a little colder here than it was in Japan. It seems good to see a few animals again. There are a large number of oxen used to carry loads, and we see quite a few dogs, something that we almost never saw in Japan. The oxen are very rarely used to pull carts but always to carry great loads on their backs. I suppose that that is because many of the roads are little more than footpaths across the hills, and a cart would be impracticable. In most places the hills are very rocy and bare, though we have seen many acres of trees that have been planted on these hills by the Japanese government in carrying out its policy of afforestation. Most of the mountains have long since been deforested by the Koreans, and the scarcity of fuel is very evident. They burn every twig and branch of the trees that they cut down, and several times we saw little children out gathering grass for fuel.

The soil did not appear to be as fertile as that of Japan, and many of the hills and mountains had been scoured down and eroded so that they were nothing but great bare rocks, without even enough soil to grow grass. The large hills around the city of Seoul, for instance, were once heavily forested, but they are now deforested and eroded so that they are almost entirely barren.

We arrived in Seoul about 8 oclock, and were met at the train by our good old friend, Mr. Niwa. We went up to the hotel and got a good nights rest in one of the nicest hotels we have seen.

Wednesday, March 22

The party started out this morning under the guidance of one female missionary and Mr. Nash, a young secretary just over from the states. We looked thru a very interesting boys school, the oldest and largest in Korea, whose principal is a young Princeton man, the son of the founder of the school. Then they were going to have a program put on in one of the other schools, whose status I didnt quite get. Lydia and I had our cameras, however, and we decided that we could see school programs some other time , and that we would be putting in our time to better advantage by going out to see what Korean life was like. We simply slipped out of the party when nobody was looking and went on a personally conducted tour of the city of Seoul, otherwise known by the Japanese as Keijo. What we didnt see wasnt worth seeing. First we stopped at the wood market, where the peasants brought loads of wood to sell. The peasants were most of them very poorly dressed and some of them were without hats, so that we could see the way they had their hair done up in a ridiculous little top-knot on their head. Their oxen had such enormous loads of wood, or rather bundles of twigs and brush, that one could hardly see the poor beasts, though at that, I dont think that the oxen were any worse off than the masters. Then there were citizens with more of this worlds goods, evidently the buyers, in their handsome long white silk robes, and the everpresent top hat, who strolled around the yard inspecting the loads of wood.

Then we wandered through the broad main streets, and past all the queer little shops where they sell everything from secondhand Singer sewing machines to fearful food concoctions. We saw them kneading a batch of dough in one place by hammering it with two immense wooden sledge hammers, the two men pounding the dough just like section men driving spikes. Every now and then we would stop in some interesting shop and try out our knowledge of Japanese. We both know how to ask the price of a thing and we also can understand the Japanese numbers pretty well, so that we had lots of fun, though our total purchases amounted to something like one yen, which is fifty cents.

After we thought we had seen enough of the main streets, we wandered back into the poorer district and walked for some time thru little hovels that were certainly not attractive as places to live. Mud floors, mud walls, the houses thrown together as thick as they could be packed, with tiny narrow lanes between that were sometimes no more than six feet wide, were perhaps the most striking characteristics of the district. We walked up a dirty little canal for some distance, and came across a group of women doing the family laundry. I dont think you would think much of their method. They would dip them into the canal, and then pull them out and soap them, and beat them on a rock with a wooden club. It surely looked like a primitive scene. The women seemed to be having a good time doing it together, though, for they jabbered and talked and laughed as they pounded the clothes.

As in Japan, everything is done by hand labor, and all carrying by manpower. Oxen, small ponies, and tiny burros are pressed into service, but the major amount of the freight carrying is done on the backs of men. These people are sure in the primitive stages of civilization, and they show it in many ways.

In the afternoon we went to a graduation exercise of some of the boys in a vocational school conducted by the Y.M. The boys were a finelooking lot and the young Korean secretary who spoke seemed to as fine a man as one would find anywhere. It doesnt seem to take very long to civilize them. From the school we went to take tea with the International Friendly Relations Association, a club of upper class Japanese whose ostensible purpose is to promote friendly relations with other countries, but who undoubtably have as one of their purposes the idea of impressing foreigners with all that Japan is doing for Korea, and to counteract the propaganda for revolt that the Koreans are undoubtably spreading. It certainly gave us a chance to meet the higher ups of Korea. Some of those present were: the head of the Mitsui Bank in Chosen, (the Mitsui is a big international Japanese bank) the head of the foreign relations dept of Korea, and his assistant, the mayor of Seoul, the chief Justice Watanabe and his wife, both of them very fine people, and several others who were all of the same class. We surely had to be on our best behaviour, for the situation is very tense here, as one can tell before you have been in the city an hour. The Koreans are still very bitter against their oppressors. On the other hand, there is no doubt and no one denys, that Japan has benefited Korea in material ways a great deal. We hope to learn more about the situation before we leave. Anyway, we were all very careful at the tea, and of course had a very interesting time with all those high mucky-mucks.

Thursday, March 23

This morning we woke up to see a real North Dakota blizzard raging outside the window. It has steadily gotten worse rather than better so far, and I am afraid that our departure for Peking which was scheduled for tomorrow morning will be delayed. We went for a walk, in spite of the blizzard, and bought a few pictures of Korean life. At noon we went with Mr. Niwa, who is head of the Japanese Y here in Korea, and had a fine guenabi luncheon. I am getting so that I can handle the chopsticks with reasonable accuracy.

Tonight we meet Mr. Cyn, the head of the Korean Y for all of Korea, and hear the Korean side of the question. It is clearly evident that we are sitting on a pent up volcano.

Friday, March 24

Last night we heard Mr. Cyn, for about tow hours, tell of some of the difficulties of the Korean YM. Altho ostensibly most of his remarks were concerned with the work of the Y, it was impossible not to read between the lines and see the whole Japanese-Korean situation in what he said. It is astonishing to find what a shortsighted policy the Japanese are following in their attempt to assimulate the Koreans. Instead of allowing the Koreans to become assimilated, they are trying to force them to become Japanese, and their policy is naturally failing. It was this dictatorial policy that led to the uprising of 1919, and altho the Japanese have slightly modified their policy since then, they are still following a policy of suppression. Naturally, in trying to follow out the principles of Jesus, the Christians have come in conflict with the powers that be, just as they have at home in their attempt to stand for Christian principles in the industrial world. The result has been that since 1912, they have been practically persecuted, and great numbers of Christians have been thrown in jail, tortured, and maltreated in various ways. We saw Baron Yun, who was in prison on a charge of conspiracy that was unquestionably a frameup, and who was tortured and terribly treated during the six years he was in prison. We have heard some very bad stories of Japans work in the peninsula, that is certain. It is a question of time whether the liberal party of Japan can gain enough power to overcome the military and develop a real constructive policy for Korea. At present, there is almost no chance for an ambitious young Korean in his own country. The service of the government is closed to him, except for very minor offices. He cannot build up a commercial concern of any size, on account of Japanese discrimination. There are no large Korean industrial concerns owned by Koreans, simply because it is impossible for them to compete with Japanese industries, backed and helped and protected by the Japanese govt. The only possible way for a young Korean to carve out a career for himself is to sell himself to the Japanese govt, and that he will not do. The Koreans are not even sending a delegate to the Peking Conference, because he would have to go as one of the Japanese delegation, and they can find no Korean who would allow himself to be called a Japanese delegate.

After Cyn had finished his talk, I asked him privately if he was much hindered by spies. When he had told me of some of the things that had happened to him, and that were happening to him every day, I surely wondered that he could keep so mellow and free from bitterness. They say that Baron Yun is even less bitter, though he has been thru things that would make most men lose all faith in a loving God. We find here in Korea that Christianity shows up best when it is under the most severe test, just as it always has all down thru the ages. Thank God Christianity is always a force to be feared by autocratic power. I hope it always will be a force to be feared by autocratic power, whether that power is found in the industrial world, the social world, or the political world.

Friday, March 24 (cont.)

Most of this day has been spent in looking out of the window, or in talking to Dave, Ken, or Dr. Tate, a fine old Korean missionary. We have been passing through great level valleys, quite intensively cultivated, dotted here and there with little hamlets of mud huts, always having as a background, either near or far away, the towering bare purple hills of Korea. In many places, were it not for the intensity of cultivation, one might easily imagine that we were in the plains of Utah. It is curious how my attitude toward the people has changed in these two days in Korea. They looked very wild and almost barbaric at first, in their strange clothes, their long hair, and their scraggly, unkempt whiskers. Now, after having seen them for a longer time, having seen Korean schoolboys, and having met some fine Korean leaders, they do not appear barbaric at all. It is surely strange how quickly the human animal adapts itself to new conditions.

Dr. Tate was very interesting, and had many tales of his missionary experiences which were very interesting. His attitude toward his work was also interesting. Ken asked him what it was that had held him out here for so many years. He replied that it was not because he particularly liked the country. Some people liked it better than America. He did not. If he had simply had his choice, he would have stayed in America, but he was fully satisfied that he had made the right choice in coming out here, for he had been able to accomplish so much more. If he had stayed at home, he could have had some influence in one church; out here he could point to fifty churches that he had organized and established himself, and he felt that the bigness of the work amply repaid him for having to live out here.

At 9:50 in the evening we arrived at Antung, on the Chinese border. We got off the train and opened our trunks for customs inspection, which was rather perfunctory. It was here that we got our first view of the Manchurians; great strapping Chinamen that would make three Japanese. They are fine big fellows. Ken had a good time trying out his rather rusty Chinese on them. They at least understood him, tho he had a rather hard time understanding their dialect.

Saturday, March 25

"There were also many Peking carts."

We sleepily rolled off the train at Mukden at six oclock this morning, and walked into a number of things that were new to all of us except Ken. Outside the station there were a good many droshkys, Russian carriages drawn by little mules or scrawny horses, with the high yoke over the horses head, and driven by big fellows who might be lineal descendants of the Manchus from their looks. There were also many Peking carts, heavy, covered, two wheeled vehicles, pulled by the inevitable mule. In our walk thru the town one of the most striking things we observed was the difference between the Japanese and Chinese treatment of animals. Horses were rather infrequent in Japan, but I never saw a Japanese beating his horse. Here the horses are scraggly little Mongolian ponies, and the way the Chinese beat them is a shame. Every driver carries a wicked looking whip, and he doesnt seem to be able to keep it still.

In our ramble about town we came across an interesting old

Buddhist temple that was built way back in the time of the Manchus. It was all in ruins, and even Ken was unable to decipher much of the inscriptions.

At 10:15 we got on to a queer little Chinese train, with compartments that open on the side, with a narrow little alley running down the side of the car. It was a pretty good train, though we immediately noticed the lack of Japanese efficiency. All day long we were passing through the plains of Manchuria, sometimes as sandy and arid looking as the Sahara desert. There was not a speck of color anywhere. The hills in the distance were bare and unforested, and the fields were a dull drab, without a sign of green, and the mud houses just matched them in color. Most of us put in the day reading and working. We generally stopped work at each station, however, to get out and watch the people. Every station was guarded by shabby grey-uniformed soldiers that we supposed belonged to Chang Tso Lin, the military chieftain who has his headquarters at Mukden. I understand that Mott had a long talk with Gen. Ghang [Chang] to try and persuade him to have his son, a young fellow about twenty-two, come to the Peking Conference.

Sunday, March 26

By the time that we had finished breakfast the scenery began to indicate that we were nearing Peking. It was still the same drab level country, but it was more thickly populated and the cemetary plots with their drab-colored mounds of earth, were much more numerous than the day before. About 10:30 we came in sight of the walls of the city, and from then on the sights were most interesting. First we came thru the outer or Chinese wall, and then thru the much higher inner wall, into the city proper. It is staggering to think of the amount of labor that must have been necessary to build such great walls 30 or

40 feet high, extending in a great rough square, about six miles on a side.

    We pulled into the station at a little after eleven, and it was pitiful to see the ragged station coolies actually fight to get a chance to carry our baggage. Talk about unemployment - you surely find it here! Jack Childs and several other men met us at the station and took us in rikshas out to the auditorium of the Peking Union Medical School, where we attended church service. That first riksha ride gave us a taste of Peking. We passed thru narrow little streets where the smell was quite strong, to say the least, past some of the most horrible looking beggars you ever saw, and then out again onto a great broad main street, where coolies with heavy carts, and riksha men and mule carts and pedestrians all fought for the right of way. We ran right into a big funeral procession, with its long rows of queerly costumed attendants bearing banners, and its large size edition of a sedan chair, in which I suppose the deceased gentleman was taking his last ride. Possibly the most astonishing part of the ride was the fare paid to the riksha men. Twenty cents Mex, or ten cents American money, for pulling us almost two miles! I don't see how the riksha men can live. And later in the day we got a ride at least as far for only ten cents Mex. It seems like a crime to pay so little.

    After church we were taken out for dinner by a young man who is teaching in the YM Commercial College here. He took Case and myself to the house where he and several other young fellows keep a sort of bachelors apartments together. It was a typical Chinese house, and surely seemed funny to we of the western hemisphere. You walk into a gate in the wall which extends all along the street, and find yourself in a little courtyard, facing a wall right ahead of you which is supposed to act as a devil screen, for the devils hate to turn corners.

You turn to one side and go thru another gateway into a smaller courtyard, with small buildings all around it. One of these the fellows were using as a dressing room, etc. To go from dining room to kitchen it was necessary to cross the courtyard! The boy brought all our food across the yard and right into what I would have called the main door of the biggest building, in one end of which the table was set. We ate with two Austrian fellows, and our young teacher friend. All the others were out seeing the Great wall of China. These Austrians had both been officers in the war, had been captured near Lutsk, and kept in a Russian prisoner camp, one of them for four years! The stories they told of their experiences simply made one writhe. They told us that 45% of the Germans who were put in Russian prison camps died, and after what they told us, I only wonder that the percentage was so small. If you want to find some one who is set against war, talk to these fellows. They had of course escaped from their camps, and by various routes and methods, gotten down to this center of the world. Some of their fellows, not as fortunate, are still up in the camps, ignorant of the fact that the war is over. The whole dinner seemed just like a dream. Think of eating dinner in a Chinese house, in Peking, talking to two of our late enemies, the Austrians, and hearing about men suffering up in Russia who didnt even know that the war was over.

After dinner we went over to the Methodist compound and heard Dr. Mott give a talk which was interpreted for a great audience of Chinese Christian students. He spoke on the purposes of the Worlds Student Christian Federation. It is amazing to find how expectant the Chinese are. The papers run long articles on the approaching conference, and every one knows all about it and expects the conference to do great things. Even our riksha men who took us to the College shouted to the men they met that we were YM people here for a meeting, though how they knew it I am at a loss to know.

When Dr. Motts meeting was over we went to tea at the home of the pastor of the Methodist church and then went to the Taylors, who are our hosts for the time being. They have a splendid home on the North compound.

For dinner I went to the home of the Gaileys. Mr. Gailey is one of the older men here at the head of the Y work at Peking. It was really a meeting of missionaries and YM and YW people. Dave and I were inveited by Jack Childs. We had a fine meal and then Dr. Mott gave a fine short talk. He looks rather tired, and I should think he would be, after the stories I hear of him.

Had a short walk home alone thru the darkest streets I ever care to travel thru at night.

Monday, Mar 27

This afternoon we went to see the Forbidden City and the Temple of Heaven, two sights that one <u>must</u> see when he is in Peking. They were very interesting and impressive, but as usual, the sights we saw going and coming were of more interest to me than any old temple. If you will climb into a riksha with me I will try and take you a little ways thru the streets. You have doubtless noticed the difference between these riksha men and those of Japan - they are younger men, they run faster, are much more poorly dressed, and much more anxious for work. Their prices are only a fraction of what they ask in Japan, and many of them seem to be in poor condition from being underfed. You never see any old riksha men, because the pace they keep up makes the life of a riksha runner only about five years after he starts in the work. Dont stop to think about that though - you wouldnt enjoy the sights. We start down Legation street at a good pace, passing the legation buildings of all the different nations, each one guarded by soldiers, and each one surrounded by a high wall.

Now we are out on one of the real Chinese streets. Here comes a cart with a great load of lumber, pulled by a most bedraggled looking trio, a pony who looks as if he had lost all hope in the world, a little burro who looks as if he never had any, and an ox who seems to be a follower of the old stoics. Behind them is a load of coal, drawn by a gaunt little mule, with scars and rope burns all over him, and urged on by a grimy coolie with a queue, with a wicked whip that is never still. But look over here on the other side. Here comes a great fat Chinaman astride a tiny burro, so small that the mans feet almost touch the ground. And the best part of it is that he has another man running behind the burro with a whip, to keep him on the trot. I wouldnt advise you to look very long at this beggar that we are passing - Im afraid that you might not sleep well. Can that ragged, warped, deformed thing holding out his hand and making a pitiful moaning sound, be made in the image of God? Of course I know that he is a professional beggar, and that he is made up to look as bad as possible, but he is also a symptom of the condition of the people, and that is what is most shocking.

Now we are getting into the shopping district, outside of the Chien-men gate and the streets are crowded. Just watch all the women you see, and notice how many of them have a peculiar, stiff hobbling gait. Then look at their tiny deformed stumps of feet, and you will see another curse of China. But look out. Here comes a drove of the long bristled black pigs that we saw from the train windows two days ago. Right down the busy city street they come, driven by two tall Manchurians with queues, and the crowds let them pass as if they were used to seeing such sights, as I suppose they are. The shops are not as clean and neat as in Japan, but they are just as interesting. However we havent got time to stop, so we wont have to bargain with the shopkeepers, and beat him down to his "last price," as they call it. We are out on one of the broader streets now, and the stream of life is not quite so compressed though it is still voluminous. But my word! Look ahead - camels! That is the first caravan I have seen in the city. They are stopping for a rest now, at one side of the street. Of all the haughty, supercilious faces, a camels is the most haughty. Even an Englishman cant beat him. After all, though, I dont know that I blame them for looking down on these people - perhaps the people _are_ worse off than the camels. The camels have big loads, but I doubt that their spirits are being crushed to the same degree as many of the people. But not all the people are as bad off as I may have given you the impression. Here come a fellow and a girl, very well dressed, very evidently college students, and without a trace of that discouraged look that so many of the people seem to have. These two represent the cream of the country, and I think that if China is to be saved, they are the ones to do it. Here we are back at the hotel again, so we get out and pay our riksha man thirty coppers, or fifteen cents American money, for the hours ride. He smiles from ear to ear, because that is half again as much as the regular rate of twenty coppers for an hours ride.

    The Temple of Heaven was old and impressive, and really reverential - the Forbidden City was massive and most interesting in its historical connections, but the people are the real thing after all.

Tuesday, Mar 28

Rambled around the city as usual this morning and in the afternoon went through the Peking Union Medical College, which is the famous Rockefeller Foundation. It is a wonderful plant. The buildings are all built in the Chinese style of architecture which makes it really harmonize with the rest of the city, and not sick out like a sore thumb, the way these American style buildings do. It is probably the finest hospital and medical school in the world as far as equipment is concerned, and is surely a tremendous thing for the education of China. Im sorry I havent time to write about the fine things inside.

Wed, Mar 29

Procession in Peking

Last night we had dinner, we being the men of the American delegation, with Jack Childs and five Chinese, leaders in YM work. We had an interesting discussion about the Chinese

Student Movement, but the most interesting part of the discussion for me was to see the way in which the Chinese worked. Two of them, Dr. Lew and Mr. Koo, were, I think, the keenest men there. All the Chinese were fully the equals of the Americans. There surely is no doubt in my mind that the Y is following the right policy in turning over the leadership of the work to the Chinese just as fast as that is possible.

We had a Chinese dinner, with about twenty courses. They eat in even a more informal way than the Japanese, putting the bowl of food in the center of the table, and going after it with their long chopsticks. We had more queer stuff than I ever hope to see again. We had preserved eggs, which had been buried for years in the dirt. They were alright, though I failed to get very enthusiastic over them. We had fish eggs, and fish, and rice and chicken, and bamboo sprouts, and various kinds of sweet dishes, and tea, and finally ended up with a lotus seed pudding. It was some feast. I dont think that I liked it quite as well as the Japanese guenabi dinners that we had. The food all seems to have a rather insipid taste, without much spice of any kind.

The only thing that I didnt like was that it kept us until midnight - at least the feast and discussions did, and as the next day was the opening of the work of the General Committee, I thought that was too bad.

Monday, April 3

Whew! These have been busy days. The General Committee met at 9:15 the morning of the 29th and has kept us almost on the run ever since. It has been one of the most enlightening meetings I have ever attended. I see now why Dr. Rutgers used to tell us on the boat that we wouldnt have a really international mind until we had been through a meeting of the General Committee.

We met in a large room here in the "Wagon-Lits," 55 of us, around four green tables arranged in a hollow square. The whole General Committee met from 9:15 - 12:30 and from 7:30 - 10:00. The last two days we also met from 2-6:30 with half an hour off for tea at 4 oclock. The first afternoons and the time after the night meeting as well as the meal hours was taken up by the meetings of subcommittees. As I was on two sub-committees I was rather rushed. A great deal of the work that we took up was simply necessary - not awfully interesting though very important. For instance we had to decide whether or not certain new student movements were eligible to enter the Federation. I was also on the sub-committee that examined the evidence and made our recommendations before it went to the General Comm. Then we had to decide what should be done this year in the way of relief work, especially in Russia. It was very interesting to hear Miss Klavin, who has just come from Russia, and Mr. Nikitin, who had just come from Bulgaria, tell of the conditions of the Russian students in Russia and the refugees in the middle-European countries. Neither of them could speak English at all well, but they certainly had the facts which were more eloquent than nine tenths of the speeches we hear.

I cant of course go thru all the business of the committee, but I will tell a little about the three high spots of the session. I think the first one was the discussion of student representation on the Executive Committee. It had been a matter of considerable surprise to me to find that of the 55 on the General Comm. there were only eight undergraduates. Four of these, of course are from the U.S. We eight undergrads talked the thing over and decided to try and see if we couldnt find some way to also get at least two students on the Executive Comm, by enlarging the Comm from ten to twelve. There were lots of obstacles to such a course, but I went around and found that India, China, and Canada would back such action as well as the countries from which the undergrads came - the U.S., Australia, and New Zealand. On the strength of that we decided to bring the thing up for a healthy discussion anyway. Of course it simply turned into a discussion of whether or not the Federation was really what it claimed to be, a student organization. It was a brisk and lively discussion, and I feel that it was very valuable, although it became evident that it would be impossible to take any definite step at this meeting. We did get a commission formed, however, to study the problem and see what can be done, reporting two years from now.

The next high spot, and this was really a high spot, was the discussion as to what attitude the student Christian Movements should take toward followers of other faiths, Hinduism, Confucianism, etc. I think that that evening was one of the most inspiring of the whole session. I know that you would have liked to hear Mr. Paul of India, tell what he believes about Christianity and Hinduism. He said that Christianity is no long being taught as being a faith that destroys Hinduism, or as an opposite to Hinduism. Christ is regarded instead, as the fulfiller of all that is good in Judaism. Somehow it gave me a new vision of the completeness and wonderfulness of Christ, to consider Him as being not only the Messiah of the Jews, but also the crown of Hinduism. Dr. Lew and Mr. Koo, in speaking for the Chinese, said that the conflict in China was not between Christianity and other religions, but between religion and no religion. From all that we hear and read in the papers, he is certainly right. There are two movements that have started in China within the past month, in opposition to the Conference. One is Anti-Christian Worlds Student Federation, started at Shanghai, which has as its main charge that Christianity is capitalistic, and that it is simply a tool of the capitalists. Although of course there is a real basis in fact of their charges, their attack is really superficial, and probably will not turn out to be of great importance. The other and more important movement is one which started at Peking and has spread like wildfire throughout the country. It is the Anti-religion movement, and hundreds of students are joining it. Their arguments in brief, are: (1) Christianity is foreign, (2) it is a superstition we are bringing to China, just when China is trying her best to get rid of superstition, (3) Christianity is an oppressor of mankind, (4) It is an ally of capitalism, (5) It is already a dying religion in America and Europe; why try and force it on the Chinese? They are putting up a real fight, and I have no doubt it will eventually be a good thing. It is already focusing attention on the Conference more than a thousand dollars spent in advertising would do; and it will make the leaders of the Conference very careful as to every step they take, because they know that they are being watched with careful scrutiny by students who are only too anxious to criticize.

The third high spot of the conference was the six or seven hours we spent in discussing the international object of the Federation. The committee on this subject had an awful time trying to frame some sort of a resolution on the subject of war that would please everybody, or that everyone would agree to. In the end we found it impossible to come to any agreement as to a resolution, but we did come to a real unity of spirit on the subject, I think. The first evening we discussed the subject, I felt really more discouraged than at any other time during the session. We seemed to see the problem from so many points of view, all of them so absolutely different that it seemed impossible to come to any common understanding. We came nearer to having a fight that night than I ever want us to come again. I really began to despair of the hope that we so casually express until we have seen other peoples, that humanity is the same the world over. By the next afternoon, however, we had found that we were all really wanting the same thing, namely to really follow the principles of Christ in regard to war, but we had certainly taken each our separate path to get there. The Indian delegation, all followers of Ghandi, the great Indian leader of the noncooperation movement, and a firm believer in the policy of nonviolence, wanted us all to take the ultimate and real Christian position in regard to war, that of complete pacifism. Most of the group felt, however, that we did not want to take any position that we were not absolutely sure that we could hold, and they were afraid that we couldnt go that far. I think we would all go as far as Miss Moncrieff of New Zealand put it; we might not have the courage to go all the way and take the pacifist stand, but if another war came, and we did participate, we would at least admit that we were doing an absolutely unChristian act in going to war, either as nations or individuals. The whole discussion was tremendously interesting, and I couldnt help but feel that we are right on the brink of a new Christian era, when we are going to quit, perhaps theologising about Christ, and begin to really practise his principles. I wouldnt be surprised if at the next Federation meetings, either two or four years from now, we might be able to have the student world come out unitedly, or at least fairly unitedly, absolutely against war. Then the world as it is had better look out, for if we begin to live out Jesus' principles along one line, we will undoubtably begin along other lines, and then the revolutionizing of the world will begin.

    Taken as a whole, the session has been a tremendous thing. All the old hands say that it has run off less smoothly, and has been a more real expression of the real opinion of the different movements than any previous meeting. I think that that is largely due to the presence of the undergraduates, and a few others who were undergrad in spirit if not in actuality. The first few days did nothing but impress me with the tremendous and fundamental differences in outlook of the different nationalities; the last few days as we have worked out and thought out and prayed out the solutions to our problems, has convinced me that the world is really one in Christ, and that is the only way it can come to unity. Frankly, I no longer wonder at the failure of the League of Nations, for I know that the only thing that kept our stormy meetings from just flying to pieces has been the fact that we have all been sincerely trying to follow one Lord. No matter how great our differences seem, we always feel that we must find some point of agreement, for there can be no truly fundamental difference between those who believe in the same Christ.

These have certainly been days that I will never forget nor will I ever forget the people. On my right sat Miss Fan, of the China delegation; on my left Mr. Galland, of Switzerland, but now going to do student work in South America. A little down the line to my right is the India delegation, the excitable but keenminded Mr. Paul, Miss Maya Das, with her beautiful Christian face, and Miss Zachariah, one of the handsomest girls on the Committee, though she is nealy as black as Prof. King. Near the center of the end table sits Miss Kawai of Japan, a splendidly Christian woman, with a heart that burns for the crimes of her government. Next to her is Dr. Mott, head and shoulders above everyone else, just as he always is in any gathering. The way he has handled the most difficult and delicate situations has been an education in Christian patience and wisdom. Then comes Mlle Bidgrain and the French delegation, the Dutch group is scattered along next, with a German and

Swedish delegate keeping them separate. Very unfortunately, the boat with the German delegation failed to arrive in time, and they have not come yet. Their place had to be taken by an old German professor who took notes on everything but took no part in the discussions. Next in order comes most of the rest of the American delegation, with Australians, New Zealanders, and Mr. Bull of South Africa to keep them separate. Then England and Canada, and that about completes the group at the four tables. Just outside the four tables were little tables for delegates from movements that were not yet members of the Federation. They could discuss, but not vote. Here sat Czecho-slovakia, Greece, the Philippines, Poland, Bulgaria, etc. I see in looking over the list at the main table that I left out the Russian delegate, Miss Klavin, who, tho she didnt say hardly anything, always put what she siad in such simple language, even tho her English was very bad, that she surely had a big influence on the group.

The language spoken was English, tho the French delegates could only understand, but not fluently speak, English. Accordingly, they usually spoke French, and had it interpreted.

The officers elected were the same as at present, with Dr. Mott Chairman, and Rutgers Treasurer.

The meetings have most certainly helped us all to attain a truly international mind.

Monday, April 10

Just a week since I have made an entry, and it surely has been a week filled to overflowing. I think that the best way for me to try and cover the happenings of the past week will be to first tell about the actual happenings, then about a few of the leaders of the conference, and finally about my impressions as to the message of the conference.

Tuesday, April 4

We were brought out to the campus of Tsing Hua College in the morning, and spent the morning and afternoon in trying to get acquainted with some of the other delegates. The campus is a very pretty one, with a small canal and a little lake right in the compound. It used to be the home of one of the princess or tuchuns, and is laid out with the most admirable taste, just suited for a college campus. In the afternoon we had a reception where we met several hundred people, and came to know two or three, as is the usual case with such affairs. The conference really opened in the evening with a good speech by Dr. Mott.

Wednesday. The program for the day was, 8:30 - 9:45 meeting in the auditorium. 10 - 11:15, forums on International Problems, Social and Industrial problems, Christianizing Campus life, Presenting Christianity to students, The student and the Church, and How to strengthen the W.S.C.F. I attended the one on Social and Industrial Problems, led by Dr. Hodgkin. 11:30 - 12:30, auditorium meeting in which the national movements gave their messages to the Federation. About six or seven countries were heard from each morning.

In the afternoon the whole conference hiked over to the Summer Palace, about two miles away. It is a splendid group of buildings, set most artistically on the side of a large steep hill, looking over a large artificial lake. The view from the highest building, looking down over the yellow tiled roofs of the other buildings, and with the little lake at the foot of the hill, is beautiful. The buildings are a little out of repair, because they havent been used since the time of the Empress dowager, and they would look much finer if they were cleaned up, but one soon learns that nothing is cleaned up in China. We were given a reception on the grounds by some of the churches and missions of Peking.

Thursday. Meetings in the morning as usual. The meetings of these first couple of days were rather heavy, though interesting. They were designed to meet the criticism of the anti-Xian movement that Xianity is nothing but superstition and has no sound intellectual or philosophical basis. There wer lectures on X and Science, X and Philosophy, X and Culture, etc. The evening meetings were on Xianizing International Relations, Xianizing the Social order, etc. Some of the speakers were Prof. Monnier of France, Capt. Monet of Indo China, (a Frenchman) Prof. Heim of Germany, Pastor Koch of Denmark, Miss Maya Das of India, Hodgkin, of England, Ex-Chancellor Michaelis of Germany, etc. It would be impossible to try and give even a sketch of their speeches, without filling up this journal. The official languages of the Conference were English and Chinese, each speech being interpreted. The Frenchmen spoke in French and had an English translation for us to follow.

In the afternoon we went out to see the Great Wall on a special train that carried the whole Conference. It was about a two hour ride up into the high hills before we first saw the wall, winding up over the top of a hill to our right. As the spot where we were was one of the most strategic points of defense, the Nankow Pass, there was not one wall but several walls, each one separated by an interval of several miles. Also dont have the idea that it is just one continuous wall, in more or less of a straight line. It branches and comes together again, curves and zigzags, and sometimes almost doubles back on itself, always keeping to the crest of the hills as far as possible. It is an immense thing, about twenty feet high most all the way, and about fifteen feet wide on top, I should judge. The wall is faced with great flat stones, the space between being filled with rubble, etc. The battlements on the Mongolian side and the lower battlement on the Chinese side, are made of mud brick, which seems to have weathered the years very well. We had a fine climb up to the highest peak in sight, climbing, of course, along the top of the wall. In places the wall went up hills considerably steeper than 45 degrees, and there it was made with steps. It is simple impossible to conceive of how the work could have been done with the appliances they must have had. How they got those great stones up hills steeper than 45 degrees, is more than I know, and when one thinks of 1500 miles of it, the amount of labor it must have taken is simply incredible. There are massive towers every half a mile or so, and gates at much more frequent intervals.

Friday. Meetings as usual. In the afternoon the conference went in to call upon the president at a reception given by him, but I didnt go, as I needed an afternoon to myself worse than I needed to see the president. Had a fine time playing baseball later in the afternoon.

Saturday. This was the closing day for the forums, and we had a busy time trying to adopt findings to present in the written reports of the conference. We all felt the lack of more time to continue the discussions we had started. I am afraid that I would have liked to differ again with the Ex Chancellor of the German Empire. He and I had a hard time agreeing, all the way thru. At 11:30 I had to speak for the American delegation, giving our message. The Russians also spoke Saturday morning, one from Eastern Russia, and one from Siberian Russia. Their speeches were fascinating, as they told of the persecution that the Russian Student Movement is going thru, and yet said that never before, in spite of hunger, and poverty, and persecution, and actual martyrdom of many students, never before had the Russian movement been so strong, or had such a sublime faith. It surely sent a thrill thru one to hear their stories from their own lips.

Saturday afternoon the sub-committee of the General Committee on the International Object of the Federation met all afternoon, trying to reach some common mind on the Christian attitude toward international relations. The discussion centered around war, just as it had in the General Committee. We didnt get anywhere.

Sunday the committee met again, and thrashed the matter over again. We simply differed fundamentally, and some of us tried our best to get the committee to issue a split report, but the chairman thought that we ought to try for a while longer to come to an agreement. Australia and India are solidly pacifist. The Indians believe that the use of force is not justifiable. The Australians do not go that far. They recognize that there is a distinct difference between police force to keep law and order, and international war as it is carried on today, with its carefully organized methods of killing men. Not only is that part of it un-Christian, but the careful fabrication of lies and half truths by the govts on both sides to keep up the fighting spirit of the people they condemn. Therefore they refuse to participate in war. The Europeans, however, almost ot a man, feel that war is often justified, and they would not sign a statement that war is wrong if they were to be shot for it. It was a discouraging split, but I feel that the fact that there is now a split, means that within a couple of generations at the very most, students all over the world will be taking the position that war is unChristian, and then we may expect some results.

One member of the committee who believed that war is often justified, was trying to make a conciliatory speech, saying that after all, we had a spiritual unity deeper than our differences. Robinson turned to me and said "How can he say that we have a spiritual unity that goes deeper than our differences, when he knows that if we all believed the same as he does, we would be shooting each other tomorrow if our govts ordered us to?" I think that puts very briefly the crux of the whole situation, and you may not wonder that at times we felt almost like throwing up the sponge.

Fletcher Brockman spoke in the afternoon, giving a good speech, though not quite up to my expectations. Mr. Harlow, from Asia Minor, and Mr. Brockman, and myself, had dinner out at the Smiths. Mrs Smith is Mrs. Goodrichs daughter. Mrs. Goodrich and Carrington were there. We had one swell meal.

The closing meeting of the conference was very good, also, though I must admit that it wasnt quite up to my expectations. I think that the only man who could have closed the conference as it should have been done was Hodgkin, but instead they had several short talks. Mr. Paul gave a splendid talk, which though short, saved the day, I felt.

There have been few outstanding men at this conference. There has been such a wealth of splendid men that it is hard to pick out a few of the best. Certainly, however, I would put Dr. Hodgkin in that class. He is a very tall, lanky man, nearly 6 feet 6, with a slight stoop in his shoulders, and a very fine Christian face. He is an English Quaker, one of the most refreshing thinkers that I have ever heard speak, and with a burning conviction that the only way for the world to get out of the muddle it is in, is to follow Christ and his teachings all the way, without compromise. He was in prison a little while in the war for his pacifist principles, and has dedicated his whole life to the abolishment of war.

Dr. Michaelis of Germany has been much in our eye, though I can hardly call him one of the real leaders of the conference, and certainly not one of the leaders of student thought. He is quite a liberal in his social ideas, not very liberal in his religious ideas, and without at all, I feel, the student attitude towards questions. I cant define that, but the difference is there.

Professor Monnier of France is one of the queerest old ducks you ever saw. I thought I would die laughing when I first saw him. He hasnt hardly a hair on his head, and he has a funny way of blinking his eyes that makes him look no handsomer. If you tied his hands he could no more talk than if you cut out his tongue. He is just like the professors you see in plays, going around always with a book in his hand, and reading it at meal times, and every chance he gets. Nevertheless, in spite of his queer ways, the old boy has some pretty good ideas, though I must say that I don't think that he represents the students of France.

Miss Maya Das and Mr. Paul have also been leading lights but I spoke about them in telling about the General Committee so I wont add anything now.

There have been many real leaders among the Chinese, but I think that probably David Yui is the only one that has been outstanding at the conference. He is a small man, very young, about thirty-two or three, but he is head of all the Y work in China, and that is no figurehead job, either.

Then the list wouldnt be complete without Dr. Mott. He stands out anywhere you put him. I cant help but wonder what in thunder the Federation and the Y are going to do without him. He is a real statesmen. He can handle men and difficult and complex situations with a master hand that makes you sit back and wonder. He isnt as original a thinker as Hodgkin, for instance, but he is a born ruler of men.

There are several clear impressions that I have gotten from the conference. First of all is the truly remarkable fellowship among the delegates from all over the world. In spite of differences of race and nationality, in spite of sore spots in the relations of many countries, never, even in the hottest committee discussions, have I seen any of the delegates show anything but the finest kind of spirit. Not only that, but it has been an education for a narrow, provincial middle westerner like myself to find what splendid men may be hidden behind different labels of nationality, or wrapped up in packages of different color. I have made a good many friends during this period, and that alone has made the conference worth while, I think.

The second impression that I have is that the conference has shown very clearly that the student world is absolutely wide awake. It is earnestly and thoughtfully searching for the Truth. It isnt satisfied with any last generation theological scraps. It wont swallow anything whole. It has a highly critical attitude, and anything that doesnt give the ring of truth is thrown overboard immediately. There is nothing that it hates as it hates any form of hypocrisy. It is absolutely frank and fearless, in facing all the problems before it. I have talked with both Chinese and Japanese students about the relations between the two countries, and I havent found one that has tried to evade the facts, and I havent found one that wasnt willing to frankly discuss the situation, as soon as they saw that I was willing to be frank, too. Furthermore, the students are entirely open-minded. They are ready to receive truth from any source, and dont consider that the revelation of God to man is a closed book, but that it is a process that is still going on. They are ready to receive truth both from inside and outside organized religion.

A third very strong impression is that the students realize that we have not, during the past, tried to live our Christianity.

We have been content with following Christ halfway. The church has always been ready to compromise with evil. They have said, for instance, that war is wrong, but they havent meant it. Every time that a war breaks out, they ahve been able to find some excuse to prove that this war is right, and we have had the horrible joke of Christian men killing each other, both saying and believing that they are following Jesus' way. I think that the present student generation, whether they will succeed or not, is going to actually try out Christs way. They may fail. Perhaps we havent got a God that we can trust all the way. Maybe Christ didnt mean it when he said that we should live entirely by the law of love, but I believe that the experiment is going to be tried, by many of the student leaders. They realize that it will mean literally the way of the Cross, for you cant go dead against the established customs and traditions of the church and society without paying the price, but I still believe that the experiment is going to be tried.

Another very strong feeling that not only I have, but many of those to whom I have talked, is that we are standing on the brink of a new day. I do not mean that in any rhetorical way. I mean it literally. The students are tired of compromising. They are tired of the present policies of the church today. They are beginning to feel that definitely and consciously, they must help bring in a new day, when Christs principles shall be not merely preached, but applied in every phase of our modern life. They realize that to reconstruct society on Christs principles means changes far more revolutionary than Bolshevism ever brought about, but they are willing to make the attempt. Do not think, either, that they are starting with any hip-hip-horray spirit that will soon fade. This conference has had no note of false optimism. It has been charged thru and thru with a realization of the terrible amount of evil, and selfishness, and hatred, that we are facing in the world, and this realization has driven us back to Christ as absolutely the only one who has a solution for the problems of the world. Every other way has been tried and found wanting. Why not take Christ at his word and try His way?

As a whole, this conference has affected me not so much thru the speeches, fine as some of them were, but far more thru the talks and discussions, and differences, I have had with the students and leaders from all the different countries. It has been a tremendous experience to find what a wonderful Christ we have, and to see that He is completely adequate to fill the needs of men and women all over the world, no matter how much they differ in background, in language, in color, in nationality. Have we a Christ who is worth proclaiming? That question can never bother me again.

A man in Northern China: "The people are the real thing after all."

April 14, 1922

We left Peking last night at ten oclock and rolled off the train at five oclock this A.M. at Shikiachuang. We had breakfast at the Hotel and took the train for Taiyuanfu. There are six of us in the party; Mr. Medard, from France, Prof. Heim of Germany, Cecil Phillips of India, Mr. Hall of Great Britain, Mr. Chen of Shanghai, and myself.

The ride to Taiyuanfu was very interesting. For the first time since we left Japan we saw green fields and trees. It surely seemed good to see a bit of color. The winter wheat looked very good where it was irrigated, though it was very poor otherwise. There were many wells for irrigation. Some of them were operated by two or four men working a large windlass, and pouring the water into the irrigation ditches from buckets; others were operated by a crude mechanism of which a blindfolded donkey, wallking in circles, was the motive power. As we began to get up into the mountains, the green fields disappeared, but the scenery was very fine, nevertheless. There were fine clear moutain streams, with little mud villages on the banks, and with crude but picturesque little mills for grinding grain, located out on islands in the stream.

Every now and then we would see donkey trains winding over the hills, loaded with coal or grain, or some other product. Once we saw a great long camel caravan, the longest we have seen yet, coming out of the great gate of one of the walled cities along the route. Those walled cities are really old China. It takes no imagination at all to see Mongolian raiders on their tough little ponies, trying to capture the city, and held off by those great massive walls, sometimes thirty feet high. The gate towers are simply immense, and they are always well situated and guarded.

The soil of all this region is the loess soil of western China - fine as powder, yet when packed, so strong and unyielding that it will not slide at all even if cut vertically. All the railroad cuts are made perfectly vertical, and they dont cave in on the tracks at all. The donkey cart roads thru this part of the country are all worn deep by the passing of these solid wheeled carts, and it is very common to see only the donkeys ears and the head of the driver sticking up above the level of the ground. We saw a couple of roads that were worn twenty feet deep and looked more like great ravines than roads. The people often build their houses in the sidehills, because of the ease of digging nice caves in this soil. Sometimes they front their cave with a brick front, which makes a peculiar looking combination.

I got off the train at Uet Hsu, where Dr. Hemingway met me. The rest of the party went on to Taiyuanfu. The doctor said that he had his motorcycle down the road a little, so we started walking, down the cart road, filled with carts hauling cotton to be shipped to Peking - providing it can get thru to Peking before Wu Pei Fu and Chang Tso Lin start fighting. I thought that I had seen dust before. I found that I had never had the slightest idea of what dust was. I stepped into the road, and went over my shoe tops in the finest floury dust I ever hope to see. You breathe it and taste it, and it colors your clothes a dull gray, and it fills your mouth and throat - it surely is the real stuff. Soon we came out on the motor road built by the Governors soldiers and the Red Cross, and then it wasnt so bad, for they allow no donkey carts on the road, and it isnt so very dusty, though there are some great bumps and ruts crossing the road. It was a twenty-five mile ride out to Taiku, and supper time when we got there. After supper, Dr. H took me thru the hospital buildings, of which there are several. We saw the opium patients who come there to be cured of the habit, and patients with T.B. and surgical cases - everything, in fact, that there was to see. They have a very fine looking Chinese woman doctor, and several nice Chinese doctors and internes, and nurses. The buildings are very nice, and are built in the Chinese style of architecture, which I think is much nicer, at least out here than our stiff American style.

We ended the evening over at the "Women's Temple," the building where all the single women stay.

April 15

Started out the day by speaking at the Chapel of the Boys School of the Oberlin Shansi Mission, about a mile away. After that I looked all around the school, and then Dr. H. called for me on his motorcycle. We rode thru the village of Taiku, and afforded pleasure and entertainment to the whole community by so doing. They sure clear the streets when the hear the old bus coming. We went into the old Chinese jail, and then into the new model jail. Both of them are in use. The old one is the filthiest, lousiest hole that I ever care to see. Twenty men were crowded into a very small room without a single window, though the door is slatted, so that a little air and light leak in. Back in one corner of that room is a barred off portion, dark as the Styx, where the worst offenders are put. The poor wretches just kotowed and grovelled on the ground when they saw us, and when we went in. I suppose they thought we could do something to help them.

The model jail was very different. The men live in clean cells, and are put to work making rugs and weaving cloth.

We went back to the mission, and Mrs. H. and little Winifred showed me thru the Girls School and the school for married women. It was all very interesting, for it was the first chance

I had had to see real mission work outside of the cities. After a swell Chinese dinner we (Dr. H. and I) started back for Uet Hsu. We got a late start, and had to go faster than the road was built for. We hit some sand a little too fast and went off the embankment. We took one other spill, too, but came thru none the worse for wear. We got to Taiyuanfu in time for supper, and then the whole team had to talk to the foreign community in a little rather informal meeting.

April 16

In spite of protest and vehement indignation, I had to lead the Easter service at the little Chinese Independent church here. It is a most interesting little group of people, split off from the Baptist mission because they were too conservative. They are nearly all young men, and a mighty fine looking lot. In the afternoon I had to talk to a group of about 150 students from the different middle schools and colleges. Medard and I were the speakers.

In the evening we were invited to dinner by Gov. Yen, the so-called "Model Governor" of this model province. He really is a very good ruler, and there is no doubt that his province is far more prosperous and better kept than any of the others. He has a good many soldiers, just like the rest, but he make them work on the roads, etc, so that they do more than simply eat up 90% of the taxes. We had a very fine dinner, and it was a good group of officials that ate with us. The governor is a nice, tubby, kindly faced amiable man, who chatted with us in a very interesting manner, thru an interpreter, of course. It seemed almost like a story from the Arabian Nights, to be sitting with those walrus-whiskered old Chinese officials, in Shansi, China! It added to the illusion to be lighted out of the Yamen, the palace grounds, by soldiers carrying immense lanterns on the end of a pole which they carried over their shoulders. The governor presented us with an autographed picture of himself. It doesnt look like him, but it is nice to have, no doubt.

April 17

Had a meeting of the Y staff at nine this morning, and then looked around the city until dinner. I spoke to about two hundred dandy Primary School boys at two oclock. They were from twelve to sixteen, and were as fine as any boys anywhere in the world.

At four Hall and Heim spoke to about 1500 soldier students from the military school and industrial schools. Then we had a reception for the teachers of the city, at which we all said "a few words," dont you know.

We had a most splendiferous Chinese feast of considerably over twenty courses at the Home of Col. Chou, one of the most interesting men here in Taiyuanfu. He has been taken away from his command by the gov., because he was getting so popular that the gov. began to fear for his place. He is a fine Christian, and has done everything for the Y here. He has his home simply full of the most wonderful curios and antiques. The feast is really too much to attempt to describe. The most interesting new thing that we had was shark fins. I thought I would bust before we finished. It really makes you feel guilty to have such a wealth of food in such a povertystricken country, and I was glad when Col. Chou said that he didnt like to have so much food when there were people who were really in need of it, and that he very rarely had such a feast, but that he did not know in what other way he could show such an international deputation the honor it deserved, so he had broken his rule.

They have all treated us royally here, and I wish that I thought we deserved it.

April 18

I have been writing the last couple of pages on the train this morning as we ride back to Shikiachuang. It is interesting looking out of the window, but I feel more in need of sleep than scenery, so I think that I will quit the clicker for now.

April 18 (cont.)

War, war, and rumors of war. Mostly rumors, to be sure, but exciting, nevertheless. When we got to Shikiachuang, we found that Wu Pei Fu's troops were being shipped to the north and that the train service was pretty much disorganized. No train had come thru from Peking for a long time, but within half an hour of our arrival a train came thru, and we took it. It was only a train of boxcars, to be sure, but we managed to get a whole car to ourselves, and made ourselves as comfortable as possible. It was lots of fun, for all of the crowd are good sports. We started about six oclock, and went to bed early, on such beds as we were able to fix up on the floor of the boxcar. The joggling and bumping of the car were not particularly conducive to sleep, but we got some rest. Since we had quite a little baggage, we kept a system of guards, and I had the watch from 10 to 12.

In spite of all the movements of troops, there is no actual fighting as yet, tho it is pretty certain to come. The pity of it is that there is absolutely no principle involved. It is simply a struggle for power between Chang Tso Lin in the North and Wu Pei Fu, who has his center at Hankow.

April 19, 1922

We arrived at Chengchow about nine oclock in the morning about as dirty as I ever hope to be. We were mighty well taken care of however, and soon had a bath and got cleaned up.

Chengchow is an industrial city, without much student work. As a consequence, we have not been very busy and we have had a chance to see what Chinese industrial conditions are like. I must admit that the sight isnt very inspiring.

The Y here is supported by the large cotton mill which is the main plant here. It has barely gotten a start as yet, and I think that the two secretaries, Mr. Zung and Mr. Smith, are going to do some very good work.

April 21, 1922

The main thing that we have seen here at Chengchow is the cotton mill. We have spoken to a few groups, but I think that I would rather tell about the mill.

It was a very interesting mill, from every point of view. We saw the raw cotton come in and watched it all thru every process until it came out finished cloth. But that wasnt what I was most interested in. I wanted particularly to see how they were solving the industrial problems that we also are facing. They employ 2000 men and women and children. I should say that over half of that number are women and children, from 12 to seventeen. The mill itself is a good modern factory. It is clean, quite well lighted, and the work for the women and children is not particularly hard. The managers, two of them, are Christian, and they are really trying, I think, to do the fair thing. They are up against some most difficult problems.

The conditions of work are not as good as the factory. It is a 24 hour establishment, and they work in two twelve hour shifts, which I do not like. The women and children also work at night, and also work twelve hours every day. They have one day off out of fourteen. They at least do not have the barbarous system of the steel mills of having a 24 hour shift when they change over from day to night work. In that respect, at least, they are ahead of America. Their twelve hours work is a steady stretch without a break, and they eat their meal while they work. No the conditions are certainly not ideal. I saw one of the women who was working the great looms, who had her baby in a big basket beside the loom - not more than a month old at the most, I dont think, and right in all that dust and noise that is worse than a boiler factory. Even the little girls, some of them tiny, pale little girls, not more than twelve years old, have bound feet, and I must admit that I didnt have an easy time going to sleep that night, as I thought of those tiny girls, working all night long, standing painfully on their crippled little feet. One almost feels like damning the whole rotten system that makes such things possible. Certainly it has got to be radically changed, and the students of this generation are the ones who are going to start the work.

The average of the pay for the mill people is $.20 Mex, big money, or 34 coppers. That amount to 10 cents gold. The boys and girls are paid $.17 Mex, or about 9 cents gold, a day. High pay! It is not very big pay even for this country, but better than many of the people get.

Many of the men and women hired by the mill live in houses built for them. They wouldnt let us see them, but from seeing the hovels that the people in the city live in, I can guess what they are like. This is the most poverty stricken city we have been in. Many of the people live in tiny mat shelters that we actually wouldnt keep our hogs in. The other houses are all of mud. I have seen a family of four living in a hut made of matting that certainly wasnt more than twelve feet long and six feet wide. It was less than five feet high in the center, and sloped down to the ground on each side. I made a mistake. I said they lived there. I meant to say that they existed there.

The Y is just getting started, but it is doing some very fine work. They have school for the sons of riksha men that is very interesting. Some of those little chaps look as bright and capable as if they were the sons of super-tuchuns.

I think that perhaps the main thing we got from our stay at Chengchow was an idea of the tremendous difficulties that men are up against when they try to better the social and industrial system, for the men in charge of the mill, for instance, really want to do the right thing, but the obstacles in the way are very great. What we need are men who are actually willing to go into business to fail, if necessary, in putting the spirit of Christ into their businesses. Even these men with all their good points, saw in the mill, only so many thousand spindles - what we need are managers who see so many thousand human personalities, every one of them with great possibilities.

April 22, 1922

The ride from Chengchow which began last night, and ended at ten oclock here at Hankow, was very interesting. We woke up this morning in a country of green trees, and grass, and waving fields of wheat and barley, which were within a month of being ripe. You can have no idea how wonderful it seemed to see country which is really luxuriantly green. Every where we have been so far, almost all the green has been there because of irrigation. It seems so good to see lots of trees, too. In many places they were getting the rice fields ready. The farmers would be wading in the mud up to their knees, guiding their crude little wooden plows, which were drawn by the most ungainly water buffaloes that you ever saw. I have gotten beyond the stage where I exclaim at every new sight, but I must say it was certainly interesting, and novel.

The country was not only more beautiful, but far more prosperous. Most of the houses are of mud brick, instead of plain mud, and they are many times larger than the houses in the north. They are somewhat cleaner, too. Sometimes one sees a good substantial brick house even in the country, even white-washed on the outside.

Hankow is a very uninteresting city to come to. It is as modern and foreign as any city we have seen. The buildings are all foreign. It is largely built up around the various concessions, British, Russian, French, etc. However you cross the river to Wuchang, and the story is very different. You run plump into the most typical old Chinese city you ever saw. The beggars, the dirt, the narrow little crooked streets, the innumerable dirty little shops, are all as Chinese as if they had never seen such a thing as a foreigner. The streets are very crowded, and it is quite an undertaking to shove your way thru in a riksha. One remarkable thing about both Wuchang and Hankow, is that I have not seen a single draft animal of any sort in either city. In Wuchang I havent even seen a cart. Everything is carried suspended from poles that men carry on their shoulders. I dont know the weight of the biggest loads, but I saw a coolie that was carrying 5 fifty pound sacks of flour, two on one end of his pole, and three on the other. He didnt seem to be working as hard as some of them.

The people are tremendously curious here. We have met another deputation team here, which came down by a different route. Miss Zachariah is on that team and the way the people stare at her dark face and her Indian costume, is a fright. It is alright for a few hours, but you have no idea how hard it gets to be simply devoured by staring eyes, for days at a time. It is hard to get used to being a foreigner.

April 24, Monday

They have certainly been working us here. Saturday night I talked to about 400 people, mostly students. Sunday morning Phillips and I lead the service at a middle school of 250 boys. In the afternoon we all talked to a crowd of 600 students. In the evening Miss Zachariah, Hall, and I talked to about 400 people at the Hankow Y. I am quite sure that I would have had to talk this morning if I hadnt skilfully eluded my pursuers. It is simply too much. I can only stand a certain amount of it. We have met wonderfully nice people here, as everywhere. There isnt a finer group on earth, I dont think, than the foreign Y men. They are princes.

Wednesday, April 26

Yesterday I went to the famous Hanyang Iron Works, and today we went thru the Yangtze Engineering Works, one of the biggest of its kind in China. They were both mighty interesting. The thing that surprised me most at the Hanyang Works was its dilapidation. It is certainly going thru hard times. The Japanese made a contract with the Chinese owners before the war to take 51% of their product at a certain price. Now they have to produce this material for Japan at a loss, because the prices have gone up so. As a consequence, the place is nearly bankrupt. It is running at one fourth of its regular production, and is pretty well run down. They have two rather old fashioned blast furnaces running. The labor conditions seemed to be pretty fair, though we didnt get such a very good chance to know what they were.

The Yangtze Works were more interesting, and in much better shape. They make everything there from railroad cars and steam launches, to cast iron stoves. The owner, Mr. Wong Kwong, was certainly nice to us, and talked to us for a long time. Outwardly he is the most pessimistic business man I have seen in China. He cant see how the govt is ever going to be stabilized. He cant see how Chinese are ever going to make decent workmen, he doesnt think that the technical colleges of China are turning out anything but white collar fellows, (which by the way is a very deserved criticism), and he is sure that if the foreigners were taken out of China, she would simply be absolutely helpless. However he doesnt act half as pessimistic as he talks. He has done more for boys than any business man I know in America. Not boys in general, but boys in particular. He has helped many poor boys thru school, he has taken likely boys into his shops to give them training, he has helped all sorts and kinds of boys, and tho of course he has had many disappointments in the way they have turned out, I notice that he is still doing it. He has done a great deal for his men. He has established a school for the children of the higher paid men, he has started a church which is really used, and which has a pastor of its own, he has put up a small auditorium where the men have movie shows part of the week, and talks the other nights, and he has done many other things to try and train his men to be better citizens.

There is no doubt that he has grounds for a great deal of his pessimism. We simply cannot imagine what these business men are up against. We think that we are bad off at home. We can have no idea of how much a stable govt means to us until we see what it is like without one. In Chengchow, for instance, Wu Pei Fu had just demanded $200,000 from the city. The week before he had demanded $20,000 and gotten it. Of course, most of it has to come from the merchants and capitalists. Here, the Yangtze Works have a fine modern blast furnace that has only been used for one year, because for two years they have never been sure that they could get a continuous supply of raw material to keep it going. If any plant seems to be making much money, along comes the military Tuchun and demands some enormous levy. The threat is always held over their heads that if they dont obey, the tuchun wont be responsible for the protection of the plant, which means that it will be looted.

However, the pitiable part of it is that when they have a chance to make money, they follow the same route that has led to every bit of labor trouble we have had in America and England, and that is going to lead us into a lot deeper trouble if we dont get a move on and do something about it. For instance, Mr. Shedd told me of one cotton mill, Japanese owned, which declared a dividend of 90% this last year; of another that declared a 40% dividend and put 10% in the sinking fund; and of one of the Hankow mills which declared a 40% dividend besides putting a large sum in the sinking fund; and that in some of these mills they had not twelve hour days for the women and children, but a fourteen hour day! God knows that we have given them splendid examples in our own history. The U.S. Steel Corporation, the Standard Oil, the packers, the Colorado Fuel and Iron - goodness knows that they have done blacker things than have yet been attempted in China, and I suppose that we cant blame heathen China too harshly for following Christian America and England. Then too we are also giving them fine examples out here. It is a commonplace out here that the most abominable conditions are found in foreign establishments. Take for instance, the case of a British owned mill here in Hankow that gets its labor by contract with a Japanese labor contractor who is allowed to make all the squeeze he can out of his job. Can you imagine any system more devilish? And yet I'll bet that some of those British stockholders back in England go to church and call themselves Christians, and wish that the church would go back to the good old days and stick to the gospel. Well, that is one point we can all agree on, for there is nothing that we wish more than that the church would begin to live, and not merely preach, the gospel.

The students we have spoken to here have seemed more interested and more receptive than any other place we have been. The only thing that I regret about the whole trip is that they havent allowed us to come in close enough grip with the students. They have spread us out os thin, that I wonder how much good is has done. We really havent come to feel that we know any of the students in the cities where we have been. That is one of the reasons that I am glad I am staying over longer.

The weather has been very hot, and will undoubtably get hotter. The flowers here in the compound of Boone University are simply exquisite. There are bushels of roses, and iris, and all sorts of flowers, and birds - its a regular bird paradise. There dont seem to be as many kinds of birds as we have, but there are lots of them. The big fat blue and white magpies are the most numerous, and are saucy and noisy as can be.

May 3, 1922

It has been some time since I have made an entry. I wont try and describe the last two days in Wuchang. Most of the time was spent in wandering around the city or playing basketball, or eating with the Shedds or the Wagners. Saturday night I took the Kiangan, a fine big river boat, for Nanking. We started off in a blaze of firecrackers, which is a common Chinese way of celebrating anything they want to celebrate. We had a quiet Sunday on board, and my only regret was that we couldnt spend more time on such a peach of a boat. We got to Nanking early Monday morning, and I went up to Ray Sweetmans house. He has been simply splendid to me all the time I have been in Nanking.

Nanking is a quaint old city. Before the Taiping Rebellion about 50 years ago, the city had a population of two or three million, but it was pretty well cleaned out, and now has a population of about 400,000. As a consequence it is a very straggling city, spread out over all the old territory, and one finds rice fields and pastures right in what should be the heart of the city. It is an immense city as far as size goes, for it is nine miles across, and has a city wall that is the largest and longest in China, twenty-two miles long, and over seventy feet high in many places.

Monday morning we went to see the big South Gate. Instead of two gates, one behind the other, there are five separate walls, and five separate gates, each one well built and easily protected. The main gate tower is at least one hundred feet above the street. It is a fine mossy old wall, grass covered on top, and in good enough shape so that it looks old, but not decrepit. From there we went to see the old examination cells, where the provincial examinatios for official positions were given. These cells used to cover acres and acres, though many of them have been torn down since the Republic in 1911. They are the tiniest cells imaginable, like little stalls, four feet deep and scarcely three feet wide. There is a place for a shelf to write on, a small high shelf, and a niche for a candle. Here the applicants used to spend three days writing their exams. When they wanted to sleep, they leaned back against the wall. A great life!

From there we went to see the big Temple of Confucious. It is a typical Chinese temple, big, impressive, with those splendid tile roofs that curl up at the corner, and with a great spacious courtyard in front of the main building. There is a real atmosphere of worship about the place. It is used twice a year by the officials. That is all.

The University of Nanking was next, and we found it one of the best equipped, and best arranged schools I have seen in the Orient. It is a union mission enterprise. They are doing quite a little along the line of agriculture, having developed a very good variety of cotton for China, and having done a good deal of experimentation along the line of sericulture. We saw their silkworms, and saw the men feeding them. They keep them in an artificially warmed room, thus raising two crops of worms a year instead of one. The worms look and act a good deal like the caterpillars I used to have down cellar. They feed them on a special variety of mulberry that they have developed here. The man in charge of the work is a very fine young Chinese.

We had dinner that night at a very nice little Chinese restaurant which served very good Chinese food, and then Ray and Mrs. Sweetman and I sat up until midnight, settling the problems of the missionary enterprise in China.

The next morning we went thru the Southeastern University, the biggest govt university in Nanking. They are building a fine new gym and a new library. You ought to have seen them driving piles for the library. They had a scaffold over the spot, and about twelve coolies stood up there and each one had a rope which was tied to a big stone. One of them would start a tune, and they would all join in on a little chorus as they heaved up the stone and let it fall on the pile. The only way they had of guiding it was a coolie down below who did his best to guide the stone. On the whole, the govt university did not have quite the equipment of the U. of Nanking. They have about 60 returned students on the faculty of the University, of which five are active Christian men. Yet they have all been for several years in Christian countries. We have certainly got to stress our foreign student work. It is the biggest opportunity we have to do real missionary work for China.

We also went to see an old bell temple before dinner. The bell is a monster, weighing twenty three tons, and the fine tone is due, they say, to the fact that the three daughters of the maker jumped into the molten metal when it was being made. I will not vouch for the truth of the story, but as a story it is very good.

After dinner we went up to see the little foreign school for the foreign children. It is a dandy little building, way up on a hill, with four fine American teachers, and they teach everything from kindergarten up thru high school. I think that they had better equipment and certainly better teachers than the average American school.

Just before supper we went for a wolk on the wall. My, but that wall just grows on one. It is a grand old ivy and grass covered monument to the stability and immobility of China. It seems as if it were simply trying to defy change. From its seventy foot point of vantage, you can see all over the city, and just outside the wall, to the east, is grand old Purple Mountain. It is lovely country.

After supper we visited with some friends of Rays who were on their way from Szechuen province to Shanghai, for the Shanghai conference. It has taken them a month to come down the river this far. They told us very interesting stories about their trip thru the Gorges of the Yangtse. Then they showed us pictures of their university at Chengtu, just as modern looking as anything we have seen around here, built in the finest style of Chinese architecture. I suppose that even way out there, it wouldnt seem as far away as it seems from here, because I've learned that you never feel far away, once you get to a place.

After a good nights sleep we got an early start this morning and I have been typewriting most of the time since I got on this train. It is fine farming country we are passing thru, with water buffaloes and rice paddies, the most interesting ingredients of the scenery. As usual, I cant get used to the sparseness of the population. This country isnt near as thickly settled as that around home.

May 11, 1922

This has been a very busy week at Shanghai and I am glad that we are on our way to Manila so that I can get time to write up the things that have impressed me during the past week.

Thanks to Mr. Geldhart, I have been able to get into the National Christian Conference of China, which has been in session this week, and I have found it mighty interesting. It is the first Chinese Christian Conference in which the missionaries have not been in the majority. This time half of the conference is Chinese, and I believe that a majority of the leaders are Chinese. The chairman, Dr. Cheng, has as difficult a job as Mott had at Peking, and I believe that he has handled it well.

The progressive, liberal Chinese, which means the majority of them, are in favor of one united church in China, without any denominations, and they want this conference to take the first steps in that direction. They propose to form at this time a national Christian council, a representative body from all the missions and churches, which shall coordinate as far as possible, the Christian work in China, and do what it can toward forming plans of organic church union. It will really be a great thing, even if they get no farther than this national council; it will at least be farther than we have gotten in America, I think, considering the dissolution of the Interchurch World Movement.

From the first, it has been fairly evident that nearly everyone was in favor of some kind of an organization to bind the work together. There have been several times, though, when it looked as if it might fall thru in spite of that. Here, even more than in America, the line between the conservative and progressive thinkers and leaders in the church is very clearly and sharply drawn, and there has been a little friction, though not as much as one might expect. The conservatives wanted to make the basis of membership in the National Council dependent on a creedal statement, which consisted of three points. Belief in (1), the deity of Christ, (2), the atonement, (3) the authority and trustworthiness of the <u>whole</u> Bible. Naturally, the liberals refused to make that a basis. In the first place, those statements mean nothing unless they are explained, - there are many theories of the atonement, for instance. (At any rate, so they tell me. Personally, I wouldn't subscribe to those statements on a bet as being the fundamentals of my faith!) The bigger reason, that they refused it was that if the council was founded on any creed, no matter how small, it made a church of it - simply a superchurch over the smaller churches, and they felt that that was simply defeating their ultimate end, and would hinder, not help, the formation of a united Chinese church. Finally, the conservatives withdrew their demand, and the council was formed by an almost unanimous vote. I think that everyone feels that a really forward step has been taken, and that perhaps China is going to be spared the denominational divisions that have so split up the church in the West.

What I have written off so quickly took several days to actually occur, since a conference of a thousand people, where they attempt to have discussion from the floor, moves very slowly, especially when every word has to be translated into another language. The chairman speaks both languages, so that he does very well. It is a funny thing to hear him put a motion for vote in both English and Chinese.

I have been very fortunate in seeing many of the schools in Shanghai this week, going with Mr. Geldhart when he takes speakers around to the different schools. I havent spoken myself, or at least only a couple of times, because I absolutely refuse to talk when there are such a galaxy of stars in town as there are at this conference. However, I have had a chance to see several of the best schools in the city.

The Shanghai Basptist College is one of the best I have seen anywhere in China. We went there to a Sunday afternoon service, and I dont know when I have seen a finer bunch of fellows. I wasnt surprised when Geldhart told me that they had their strongest association there. Sunday morning we went out to the Makteer Girls School, where Prof. King preached to the girls and to a faculty composed of mostly southerners. My, but it does my heart almost as much good as it does Willis, to see how surprised they are to find a negro who is really considerably above them in intellectual attainments, and who is just as much of a gentleman as anyone. The Chinese girls were a finelooking lot, very similar to American girls, I think, in spite of the fact that they wear pants, and high-necked jackets, instead of short skirts and low necked waists. Some of them had their hair bobbed, which goes to show that they are very similar. I certainly realize the difference between the Chinese and Japanese, as I see them here together in the same city. The Japanese women, for instance, are much prettier, much <u>cuter</u>, than the Chinese; but you never see a Japanese woman that looks as capable as many of these Chinese women. The same is true of the men.

The Chinese have the stability, the substance, the <u>stuff</u>. They arent as polite as the Japanese; they arent as refined, as a general rule; they arent as anxious to please; but they are there with the goods.

One of the most interesting schools I have visited, and one of the things that drew out the remarks above was the Japanese University here. For years it has been here, literally a hot-bed for Japanese propaganda, and a school for men who were undoubtably intended to go into business and into the service of the Japanese govt, here in China. Within the last six months, Geldhart has been able to get some outside speakers in, and widen the outlook of the students, and cut them out of their isolation, get them in contact with highclass Chinese, and simply cut the nerve of all that the govt is trying to do thru this school. The present president, who has been in office about a year, is a Christian, and Geldhart got him to come to Peking. Altogether the Y has simply changed the whole school from a hot-bed of the worst kind of aggressive nationalism, to a real school for developing an international mind. The only trouble is that they are afraid that the Japanese govt will step in and stop the Y work. I expect that it will if it learns just what they are doing. Personally, I think that it is the finest piece of work that Geldhart is doing at the present time.

On the other hand, we went to one English school, where they are having very tough sledding, because of the almost hostile, and certainly stupid attitude of the English principal. One funny thing happened there. This afore-mentioned principal, introduced Prof. King as an <u>Indian</u>. Whether he didnt know any better, or what was his idea, I dont know. Willis soon set the boys right, at any rate. As a city, I dont like Shanghai. It is port city, and as usual, port cities have a bad reputation. It is the first city I have seen where they have had to have signs warning the people to look out for pick pockets. It is the first city where I have been unable to trust the riksha men, and it is not what one would call a good city in any way. It is very modern, with streetcars - the first I have seen since Tokio, I think, and with modern department stores, owned by the Chinese, and with a good police system. The police are all great big Sikh policemen, with long beards which they braid and stick up under their great red turbans. They look very ferocious at first, but seem to be a very good natured bunch.

The city is growing very fast, and I have seen more buildings and factories going up than in any other city, I guess. I hope to be able to go thru a factory when I come back.

I havent been spending all my time in such serious pursuits, however. One night we went to a fine concert with a chorus of 220 Chinese young men and women, about as fine a chorus as I have ever heard. Fine young fellows and girls, too. One other night we went to a Japanese restaurant and had a guenabi. Several noons I have had lunch with some members of the American delegation. One noon Ruth, Willis, and I had lunch togehter - members of three races, but all Americans. The people around us always get a liberal education watching Willis. Every time I have eaten with him this week, there have been groups of people who nearly ruin their eyesight staring at us.

Then last night we had a reunion of the American delegation. It sure seemed good to have the whole bunch together again, but mighty tough to have to be the first one to bust it up. As usual when we all get together, it was a hilarious time, and we busted up about eleven, because Dean Conrad thought that we had had a long enough party.

This morning I hustled around to get on the boat before ten oclock, the scheduled time of sailing. Some of the delegation were down to see us off, but they didnt stay until the boat sailed, because we found out that it wouldnt start before twelve. As a matter of fact, we didnt get started until one-thirty, and then it was so late that we couldnt get out of the river at Woosung, the city at the mouth of the river, because the tide was too low. So here we are at six oclock in the evening still within a few miles of our starting point, waiting for the tide to come in.

It is a splendid big boat, much nicer than the Taiyo, tho not quite as big. It seems good to have a crew that speaks and understands English, and these American officers look good to me. I'm still quite national-minded, you see.

Sunday, May 14, 1922

All day we had been steaming down the coast of the island of Luzon, very fine tree-covered hills forming the backbone of the island, and about two oclock in the afternoon came into the famous Manila Harbor, where twenty four years and two weeks ago Commodore Dewey sank the whole Spanish fleet and brought the Philippines out of the hand of Spain. If it was as hot that day as it was today, I pity the poor sailors, for it is a terribly muggy day. This is the hottest time of the year in this part of the world, and I certainly believe it. We got off the boat, and got in touch with Mr. Turner, the Y secretary here, and he came and got us in his car, and we were invited out to dinner by Dr. Steinmetz, who knows Ken, and then after supper we had to speak to a Young Peoples meeting, and then came back to the boat and went to bed.

Wednesday, May 17, 1922

These have been tremendously interesting and educational days, and also mighty hot ones, too. Monday Dr. Steinmetz took us

MY TRIP TO CHINA

around to the Mary Johnstone Hospital, and one other, both of them mission hospitals. We drove thru quite modern streets, rather like an American city except for the people and the numerous carabao, the great water buffaloes that they use for hauling everything under the sun. The people are very small compared to Americans, most of them dressed in American clothes except the women, who have a curious dress that I am not quite equal to describing, but which is quite good-looking.

The hospitals were both of them full to overflowing, and could use twice the space if they had it. The Mary Johnstone Hospital is for women and children. I never again want to see such children as I saw there. The amount of starvation and malnutrition is something frightful. It is largely due not so much to poverty, for there isnt such a great deal of that, but simply to ignorance. We saw there poor little kiddies whose legs and arms were simply bones with the skin hanging on in folds and flaps. I have seen lots of sights, but this was honestly the worse I have ever seen. There was one little girl eight years old, who weighed 25 pounds. Her case was complicated by

"The amount of starvation and malnutrition is something frightful"

129

tuberculosis. I wish that I could forget some of the things I saw there.

We talked for about an hour with Dr. Laubach, head of the new Union College and Seminary in the city and had lunch with him. He was a mighty interesting man, and he certainly knows the islands. He gave us a lot of interesting dope, largely about religious work in the islands.

In the afternoon we went thru the old walled city, wandering around and looking into the old Spanish churches, of which there are a number in the city. On the whole, the city reminded me more of the old Creole portion of New Orleans than anything else I know of. It is a typical tropical city, and no one works very hard, except the carabao. After having been here three days I begin to sympathize with them. (the people, I mean, not the carabao.) The children use more or less clothing, usually less. Many of them look like the add "I wish my mother would use Wool Soap." Even the older people certainly use an almost irreducible minimum of clothing, and I dont blame them. It is the hottest heat I have ever been in. You can almost pick up a chunk of air and wring water out of it.

That night we had dinner at the Turners, and got a good nights sleep on the boat, in spite of the heat, thanks to our electric fan. Tuesday morning we went thru the American Y and the Filipino student Y, and then had a talk with Mr. Corpus, a Filipino who is head of the Bureau of Agriculture.

In the afternoon we went out to Fort McKinley, where 4500 troops are stationed, and looked around the camp a little. It is a mighty nice place. On the way out we stopped at the ruins of one of the largest old Spanish monasteries. It was set on fire by the Spaniards when they had to get out because it was being bombarded by the American fleet in the river. It was an impressive old ruin, and very mysterious in many ways. There were so many queer little rooms that we couldnt imagine what they could have been used for. For instance, the most mysterious was a box shaped little building in the cloister, all overgrown with weeds now, which had only two windows, which used to be barred, and no door at all. We climbed in thru one of the windows, and found that three fourths of the place consisted of a deep pit full of water, with only a little square platform in one corner. Then we looked up, and I'll admit I kind of gasped for there above the water was a round hold in the ceiling, just about the size of a large manhole. Whether they let men thru the ceiling and dipped them in the water, or whether they quietly dropped obstreporous heretics thru the hole into the water, I dont know. If the latter, and the Spanish friars were certainly capable of doing such things, why have the small dry platform in one corner. You could certainly let your imagination run wild in that old monastery, I must admit.

Then Mr. Turner took us about twenty miles out into the country, past little hamlets, or barrios, as they call them, where the houses, such as they are, are all put up on stilts, partly, I suppose to make them dryer and cooler, and partly to make room for the animals to sleep under the house. You can imagine what a beautiful perfume that must make in the house. The houses themselves are simply made with a bamboo framework, and thatched with the leaves of a sort of palm. The people have little gardens right near their houses, and their bamboo fenced yards are usually full of banana trees. Their rice fields are all outside of the village. The village street is sleepy and quiet, with an occasional carabao plodding along with his cart, or a dusky beauty walking carelessly along with an immense basket balanced on her head. The men seem to spend most of their time taking siestas. In fact, life is just one long siesta out here for the average native.

His living comes very easily, and he takes everything else the same way.

After this interesting plains country, we got up into the hills where the scenery reminded me somewhat of that outside of Honolulu. Finally we reached our destination - the church of Antipolo, one of the sacred spots of the Philippines, where there is a large old Spanish church, containing a very famous image of the Virgin, which is supposed to have miraculous power and which is one of the richest images in the islands, because of the gifts which have been heaped upon her. The church was crowded with young people, but almost none of them, one noticed, were young people of student age. That kind have almost without exception, drifted away from the Catholic church. We were told later, by Judge Santos, a Filipino Catholic, that 90% of the people did not have the slightest idea of the significance of the service nor did they have any knowledge of the Catholic faith. It is simply a superstitious worship - typical medieval Christianity. The church was tawdry and musty and dirty - nothing in it that would give the idea of worship or reverence to our minds, but the people evidently thought they were getting something out of it. After the service the image of the Virgin was turned around, and the people all filed past her in back of the altar, kissing her robe, etc. We got them to lift her veil, and let us see her face. It was certainly rather a shock to find that her face was a very dark brown, and distinctly Spanish in feature - not at all the type that one usually sees in Catholic pictures.

If we needed any further proof than what we had heard about the decadence of Catholicism in the islands, we surely found it here. They are just the picture of what I read last semester about the medieval Catholic church. The priests are notoriously immoral, immensely wealthy, and until the American occupation were hated with an intense hatred by all the people for their oppression. The people, however did not dare risk going against them, partly because the priests were backed by the govt, and partly for fear of what the priests could do to their souls. All of the splendid churches and monasteries that one finds everywhere, were built by forced labor, without pay. No wonder they could afford to build so many of them!

We had dinner that night at the Steinmetz' again. Wednesday morning we had a long and mighty informing talk with Judge Santos, head of the Bureau of Justice of the Islands. We talked largely about the independence of the islands, and the arguments pro and con.

Then we went over to see Col. Johnston, who is on Gen. Woods staff, and acts as his personal aide and advisor. He gave us the other side of the question of independence, and some very startling ideas about our policy in the Philippines. It was all in confidence, however. At first he wasnt inclined to really express his opinion, but Ken very skilfully drew him out, and before he ended, he was certainly frank enough. When we finished he said that perhaps the General would like to see us. He went in to see, and in a few moments we were called in. When we went in Gen Wood was sitting in a big highbacked chair before his flat topped desk, which was perfectly empty. He looks older and stouter, than his pictures, and his face is rather more wrinkled and older than one would expect. Johnston had evidently primed him as to our conversation, for he started right in where we left off, after a few preliminary words, and told us how little the American people knew of the importance of the Philippines as a naval and commercial base. He also told us some other things about what he considered the blunders of the Washington conference, and somewhat of his attitude toward independence, which were confidential. He speaks with a good deal of force, but rather quietly and incisively. He shows his army training in the easy and accomplished way with which he now and then embellishes his conversation with picturesque phrases. He says "the devil" and a "hell of a mess" and other phrases of like nature in a way that seems very natural to him, and therefore in a way that is not offensive at all. He certainly impresses one as being sincere and honest, and profoundly patriotic in the best sense of the word. However, if the American people knew all that he told us, I think that there would be considerable of a reaction. The average American is somewhat optimistic about the future of international relations - but one certainly cannot accuse these men of that attitude. After hearing them, it certainly gives a person a chance to wonder if after all, civilization as we know it may not be headed for extinction within the next couple of generations. I tell you, the world is not going to take up the Christian method of settling disputes between nations because it wants to, but because it is going to be suicide if it doesnt.

We had lunch with Judge Kamys, one of the more conservative, but also one of the levelest headed of the Filipino judges. He added to our ever increasing stock of information about the islands. We talked quite a little about the progress of Christian work in the islands. It is mighty evident to all of the people who are doing any real thinking on the subject, that unless the Protestant churches unite, they are going to let slip the great opportunity that they have at the present time. The Catholic church is losing the people by leaps and bounds, but the Protestant church is not at all keeping up in gathering those that are deserting the Catholic church. If they dont look out, the same thing will happen as happened in Japan. The Japanese wanted the Protestants to unite, and when they wouldnt, they busted away from the missionaries almost altogether, and formed their own church, which is naturally very weak, and not doing near as good work as it would if it had the missionary help and support during this struggling period.

After lunch we did a few things that had to be done, and then waited while a rainstorm came and went, and then went down to the boat, and got under way at five oclock. It has been far more interesting here than I had supposed it would be. It is certainly true that the American people have no conception of the strategic importance of the Philippines as a naval, commercial, and missionary base. America is making the experiment here of trying to teach an Oriental people the best things in Western civilization. If she succeeds, and the missionary work will be responsible for a large share of the success or failure, it will have a tremendous effect on missionary work in China, Japan, and India, and it will have a great effect on the colonial policy of Great Britain in India, and Japan in Korea. If we keep faith with the Filipinos, and give them their independence as we have promised, that will have a great effect too. We have certainly been fortunate in the people that we have seen, thanks to Mr. Turner, who simply put himself out to see that we got in touch with the best people on the island. I surely am lucky to be traveling with Ken, because of course I wouldnt be able to get into a quarter of the places, or see a quarter of the people that we are seeing. For instance, when I talk with the people on the boat, and hear what they have done in three days, I realize how we have gotten more real insight into the problems of the island than they would get if they stayed three months, and we have done practically as much sightseeing, too. I wish I knew why I am always so lucky. It seems as if I were always on the inside, by some hook or crook or accident, whenever there is anything of real interest going on. I am having opportunities that competent men would give a years pay to have. Yet they just fall into my hands. It means a big responsibility.

Wednesday, May 24, 1922

It has been some time since I have written up my journal, and I will try and fill in the blank days in at least a sketchy manner. We arrived in Hongkong early in the morning of the nineteenth, and came on shore soon after breakfast, bidding the Empire State goodby for the last time. We were in Hongkong for the rest of Friday and Saturday until 5 oclock. On the whole, that was long enough. It is a very pretty city, set at the foot of a great peak which overlooks the city. At night especially, when everything is lighted up, it sparkles on the side of the hill, like a great Christmas tree. It is a fairly typical port city, nicer, however, than Shanghai. It is quite semi-foreign, and has fine broad streets, and some pretty parks and drives. It isnt nearly as large as one would expect, though nearly 600,000 people are crowded into it. The city being on the side of the hill, it seems as though going around the city consisted mostly of going up and down steps. The main method of conveyance is the sedan chair, usually carried by only two men.

We looked around the city, saw several of the mission schools and hospitals, and had two very interesting visits with Catholic fathers doing mission work here in the city.

Saturday night we went up to Canton by the night boat, arriving there early in the morning. Mr. Henry, president of the Canton Christian College, met us at the boat, and we took a drive around the city in a car. It was a mighty interesting drive, for several reasons. This is the first Chinese city where I have seen evidence of a real civic pride and a good city government. They have torn down the old walls and filled up the moat, and have built fine broad streets where they have removed the old landmarks. They are building a fine big city park right in the center of the city, and a little outside the city they have made a nice little park around some fine monuments to the seventy two men who were responsible for the 1911 revolution, and who were shot by the government.

We spent the rest of the day until 5 oclock out at the C.C.C., of which I will tell later, and then came in to the home of Mr. Lerigo, one of the Y. secretaries, where we stayed for the night.

In the morning we first went thru the Hospital for the Insane, which has about 700 patients. It was rather gruesome, and sort of gives one the creeps, but it is a mighty fine piece of work, and it is the only thing of its kind, either mission or governmental, in all China! The customary Chinese way of caring for a violently insane person is to chain him up, and simply feed and clothe him. They have one patient who was kept tied by a chain around his neck, for sixteen years. No wonder he was crazy, eh wot?

Then we called upon the consul, and tapped him for what information he had upon the government situation. Like some of the other consuls we have talked to, he is very pessimistic. He thinks that the southern govt is no better than the Peking govt, and that it will in all probability collapse within a short time. He says that the govt doest extend ouside of Canton, scarcely, and that the bandits thru the province and the pirates on the river are worse than they have ever been. From what he told us they are pretty bad, alright.

Then we were fortunate enough to hear the other side of the case when we had dinner with Mr. Frank Lee, head of the department of foreign affairs for the southern govt, a mighty fine Chinese who used to be a Baptist minister, but went into govt service at the time of the revolution. He will admit most of the things that Mr. Houghton said about the southern govt, but he also sees some things that the consul did not. For instance, he says that there has been a steady growth in national spirit and a growth in allegiance to the idea of democratic govt, ever since the revolution, and that with time the govt is going to get on its feet.

Sun Yat Sen isnt as popular as he used to be in this part of the country. He had rather lowered himself on quite a good many occasions to play politics, and the men here no longer regard him as quite so much the savior of his country as they used to. His expedition into the north at the present time is largely a political move, from all that I can hear. He hopes to get his army thru to the Yangtse, and then he will have all that newly acquired territory between Canton and the Yangtse as a "talking point," as the Chinese call it, in his negotiations with the north.

There is no doubt but that political affairs both in the north and the south are in a terrible muddle at the present time. The southern government at the present time is probably the weakest in a military way, and probably in a financial way, for it has issued several millions of unsecured notes, but the policy of the southern govt for a constitutional govt is the one that will probably win out in the long run, whether this particular group of men win out or not.

During the rest of the afternoon we looked around the city. It is a very typical Chinese city, once you get off the few broad streets. We went thru one street where it wasnt even possible for a sedan chair to go, and in one short section of it, two men couldnt even pass. It wasnt just a back alley, either, though it wasnt one of the important streets.

That afternoon Ken took the boat for the Portuguese settlement of Macao, down the river, but I wanted to see more of the C.C.C. rather than any old historical place, so I went out to the Henry's for the night.

The college campus covers three hundred acres, and they have, I think, the finest buildings and equipment, (as well as the finest fellows) of any mission school I have seen yet. They have a fine college group, of two hundred students, and a middle school and primary department that bring the total up to 750. You see out here "College" usually means everything from kindergarten up, and often it is more kindergarten than anything else. This has a real college though, and its standards are accepted by the colleges of the U.S. as being on a par with their own, which is also unusual.

They have the finest student Y.M. work that I have ever seen either in China or America, and that is why I wanted to spend another day out there, largely. I talked to five or six of the students who are running it, and got all the dope I could. They are running five free schools for farmers' or village children, and they are running a night school for workmen, and they have a voluntary group of students who go out to help the govt primary teachers in the neighboring villages, and they have many Sunday schools for the village children, and they a primary school that they are starting for the children of the boat people, and so on almost ad infinitum, besides all the regular meetings and Bible classes, etc, that the average student association has. Do you wonder that I went back for another day? Believe me, they have a splendid group of young fellows who are back of the work. Also remember that all this work is managed in a college of two hundred, (though of course the middle school boys help), and that it is all done by the students themselves, as they havent been able to support a paid secretary for several years. They raise all their own finances, too, and the average pledge last year was $4.40 Mex, which looks as big, if not bigger, than the same amount in gold, to an American student.

They have a very fine agricultural college there, much finer than anything I have seen. They are doing work along the line of sericulture, dairying, hog raising, poultry, vegetables, staple crops, etc. Since nearly all the work they are doing is entirely pioneer work, it is exceptionally valuable.

In the afternoon it set in to rain, and it sure rained. I got wet coming over to the city, but it really doesnt matter in this climate. You could wring water out of your clothes any time, so what difference does it make whether it is rain water or sweat.

Last night I came down the river in a pretty good boat named the Kinshan. All these river boats carry quite a guard of turbaned Sikhs, with repeating rifles, in order to avoid any unpleasantness from the pirates. Many of the great big old junks are armed, some of them with small cannon, that look as clumsy as the boats themselves. Practically all the Chinese boats pay a "kumshaw" to the pirates in order to secure immunity. Of course, there is really not the slightest danger, (only one passenger boat, I believe, has ever been attacked) but it makes a nice romantic sounding tale, so I have put it in.

Today we have been keeping close to the hotel. Ken has been kind of layed up, poor fellow, and I have been working, reading and resting. We thought our boat went north today, but find that the date on our ticket is wrong, and that she leaves tomorrow, if the launchmens strike doesnt hold her up. They have a typhoon warning out, too, saying that there is a typhoon within 60 miles, so that that may also delay us. You see I could make up quite a hair-raising story, with typhoons, pirates, bandits in the back country, strikes, war, political disorder, and Ken sick abed, but since I am a little too truthful, I am bound to say that we are probably just as safe as if we were at home, and Ken will probably be well tomorrow. Meanwhile, the coolies outside the window chant away as they swing past with their heavy loads. They arent worried, and neither am I.

Saturday, May 27, 1922

Here we are still in Hongkong, I in the hotel and Ken in the hospital. He is getting better, but rather slowly, and I expect that we will be in town for at least three days more. He had dysentery on his last trip out here, and this seems to be a mild return of it. It is too bad he had to get sick here. It is one of the most uninteresting towns we have struck, and we also know very few people here, so that it isnt an awfully exciting time I am having. I wish we were up at Canton. Hongkong is about as provincial a city as I have ever seen. In their newspapers nothing but Hongkong news is printed. I dont suppose there has been a total of one column of U.S. news in the five days we have been here. Even the North China news is very scanty. They had chucked off in one inside column what may very possibly prove to be the most important bit of news in China since the Revolution, namely, that Wu Pei Fu, being now of course the master at Peking, is planning to call together the Old Parliament of 1913, is trying to reconcile Sun Yat Sen, and is suggesting Li Yuan Hung for president as a man who can reconcile both parties. If he can put those things thru, it will reunite China under one govt, and perhaps do away with her civil war for some time. Incidentally Dr. C.T. Wang told Ken when we were in Peking that that was what he thought Wu Pei Fu would do if he beat Chang Tso Lin. I expect that C.T. had quite a little to do with formulating that policy, too. You see, the South will not consider uniting with the North unless they recognize the Parliament which was illegally dismissed several years ago, and which fled to Canton to set up the southern govt as the only legally constituted govt in China. So it may be that this propositioin of Wu Pei Fu's, including as it does the recognition of the Old Parliament and the suggestion of a strong moderate like Li Yuan Hung, may really be very important. I sure hope it works out.

No shipping has been going out of this port until yesterday on account of a typhoon which has been moving northwest from Manila, and also partly on account of the launchmens strike. I guess it is becoming normal again, tho. The Empire State left yesterday, and the Pinetree State will be leaving Wed, so you ought to get lots of mail.

I forgot in my last entry to say anything about the river life here in South China. It is one of the most interesting things I have seen. Thousands of people dont know what it means to spend 24 hours on land. They form a kind of separate caste from the land dwellers, and they live on their boats all the time. It is an inexpensive life, and they earn a little money by ferrying people across the river, and doing a little freight work. I have seen five and six people, a whole family, living on a little covered sampan not more than twenty feet long and six feet wide. How they do it is a mystery. They have a little place in the back for a fire to cook their food, and they sleep on the bare boards, with a wooden block to put under their necks for a pillow. They often have a brood of little chicks in a tiny yard on the boat, and on the larger boats they often have a dog. They dont have to worry about space to keep their property. Their wardrobe consists of the clothes on their back, their cupboard is a place big enough to hold a bowl apiece and an iron bowl for cooking, their washtub, and bath, and dishwashing sink, and toilet, are all found in one place - the river - and that is about all there is to their lives. The bareness of their existence must be beyond comprehension.

Wednesday, June 7, 1922

Since I last made an entry, several things have happened. We left Hongkong on the 1st, Ken feeling rather under the weather, but just about able to travel. We came up the coast on a little freighter, the "Yusang," and arrived at Swatow last Friday afternoon. We stayed at the Baptist compound while we were there and have had another splendid visit at another very interesting place.

Swatow is a rapidly growing port with a population of about a quarter of a million. It is not an old city, but has sprung into prominence, as it were, within the last fifty years. The old city of which it is the port entrance is Chowchowfu, about 30 miles up the Han River. Swatow is located in a very strategic place for a commercial city, and it is no wonder it has grown. It is located at the point where the Han River empties into the river locally known as the Kichang River, and it is also only a few miles from the coast, and all but the largest liners can come right up and anchor at the city. It therefore serves as the mouth of the funnel for all the trade of the two valleys, and will undoubtedly develop into an important port. Then when they can connect Canton and Swatow with a land route it will be very effectually cut Hongkong out as a port, and that is the dream and hope of every Chinese. Hongkong is certainly not a popular city.

Right across the river from the city, the Baptist people have their work located on a rocky promontory, in a really splendid location for a boarding school. They have a primary, upper primary school, and an academy. Altogether, counting in their girls school, and their kindergarten, they have almost a thousand students at Kokchea, as the place is called. There are about 350 in the academy, which is a pretty high grade school. They are building new buildings on the hills, and are expanding in numbers just as rapidly as they can make room for the pupils. There are 21 foreigners teaching in the school, so that it makes quite a little foreign community. It was very evident that the whole school was much more foreign in its administration than the schools at Canton, or Shanghai, or Nanking. I didnt quite appreciate the reason, though, until I went up to Chowchowfu on Tuesday.

It was a delightful ride up there, even though it was drizzling. When I dont say anything about the weather these days, you may assume that it was raining. It does more of that than anything else. However, the ride was very fine. All the rice is headed out, and looks very fine, because it is so carefully weeded and cultivated. The sugar cane isnt so very far along, but there is quite a little of it, and also Chinese hemp, and all sorts and kinds of smaller garden truck. The ponds are full of ducks or geese, the latter often being watched by a little goose girl, with her great broad wicker-work hat, and her rain coat of woven palm leaves. The villages we passed looked very prosperous, and beggars are an unknown thing all thru this part of the country. All the houses are made out of a composition which is really a sort of concrete or hard mortar, and one sees none of the mud huts or mat shelters that served for houses in the north.

There were lots of interesting things about the city of Chowchowfu itself. We saw two Confucian temples with images of Confucius in them, which is a very rare thing, there being only three or four such in all China. Most of the Confucian temples have only tablets to the memory of Confucius and some of his most noted followers. We also saw a small public library, which has been in operation for about a year and which shows that altho Chowchowfu is at least a thousand years old, it still can learn new tricks. The local govt is also widening the streets. We also saw the chamber for the legislative assembly for this district. They may have such things in other cities, but I did not know that they did. I think that this is one of the few places that is really being governed with a semblance of representative democratic govt.

Another thing that I learned was that there was such a thing as big business in old China. In no other city had I seen anything but the old style of little domestic handicraft shops or the new style of modern industrial plants, but here in this Fu city I saw great warehouses and wholesale houses that were handling the produce of the valley and were doing no retail business at all. Most of them are family concerns, not stock companies, for as yet the Chinese havent developed the type of honesty that is necessary for the carrying on of a corporation. It was a surprise to find these old houses doing business on such a big scale, however. The city is really a very rich city, tho of course one would never guess that walking thru the narrow, filthy, smelly little streets. There is really nothing that can compare to the odor of a Chinese city after a rain. It is unique - to say the least.

Of course I went thru the Baptist mission work in the city. They have a school that goes from kindergarten up thru upper primary, and have about 300 pupils crowded into quarters that are entirely too small. They certainly need money for improvements and new buildings. I noticed even more here than at Swatow, that it seemed to be a foreign piece of work, and I took pains to find out why. It is very simple, but was very enlightening to me. The work in this whole valley among the people who speak this Swatow dialect is not old enough yet so that the men they have trained are coming back into the work. For instance, of ten teachers in their primary and upper primary schools, which correspond to our grades, they have only one who has had the equivalent of a high school training. Naturally, you arent going to be able to pick a Chinese principal for the school out of that crowd. It will be some years yet before any of their men come back college trained. When I see the tremendous difference in the amount of Chinese leadership between places like this and Canton, for instance, and then think of the fact that in a few years this place will have as much Chinese leadership as Canton, I see why even the conservative think that the missionaries job will be over in China within forty or fifty years, and some would place the estimate at twenty years.

There are two men and their families in the Baptist work at Chowchowfu, and about the same number in the English mission. It is a little nearer to being an outpost than most of the missions I have seen, tho it is not an outpost. I want to see at least one out-station before I go home. That doesnt necessarily mean that I will have to go a long ways from the cities. I hope to find one in some of the smaller cities around Shanghai. The more I see of these smaller city stations, the more I admire the people who are in them. Some of them may be very conservative in their theology, but I certainly admire their nerve in sticking right on their job, even though it is almost impossible to see any real results. They are doing wonderful work. By no means are they always conservative in their theology, either. Hildreth, at Chowchowfu, was a Union Seminary man, and a peach of a fellow, about 35 years old, perhaps. Baker was a little older, and tho he comes from a very conservative seminary, Louisville, is as openminded and tolerant as one could wish. The mission stands very well with the officials here for several reasons. Baker and an Englishman once stopped a war which threatened to make the city the center of its action, and naturally, they feel rather agreeable for that reason. Then Hildreth and one of the

Englishmen kept a band of Chekiang soldiers from looting the city a couple of years ago, and that helps, too.

I came back from Chowchowfu this morning and bid farewell to all the people here this afternoon. It surely is a wonderful experience to come into a port like this, not knowing a soul, and to leave with several people that you can really call friends, and a great many fine acquaintances. There is a splendid group here in Swatow. I enjoyed especially meeting Paul Cressy, and Miss Smith, because they are young people who have just come out here, and they gave me some very valuable first impressions of mission work as it had exceeded some of their expectations, and disappointed others.

We are now on the "Haiching," bound for Foochow. Altho only a little way out into the ocean, there is a nasty wind picking up, and the officer is wondering whether we are going to get caught in a typhoon. Well, we are out here for experience, and we usually seem to be getting it, so we may get this. I havent completely gotten my sea legs yet, and this roll gets my goat just a little bit when I sit still, so I think that I will go up on deck and walk until dinnertime.

June 8, 1922

Well, our wind didnt develop into a typhoon after all, tho it was fairly rough. It was a great sight to watch the little fishing junks trying to get to shore from way out five or ten miles where they had been fishing. They would sink almost out of sight in the trough of the waves, and then be lifted way up on the crest, with the dripping prow just balanced in empty space, and then they would plunge nose down into the next wave, raising a cloud of spray that would hide the whole boat for a second or two. I sure admire the nerve of their skippers.

This morning we arrived at Amoy. We wound around several fine islands into the harbor of Amoy, which is itself located on an island. As the ship was only going to stop three hours, we had very little time to see things. We went off onto Kulangsu, the island where most foreigners live, and saw some of the mission schools, and had a long talk with Mr. Elliott, the Y secretary there, but we didnt get over to the city itself, partly because our time was so short, and partly because the plague was a little worse there than in most of the cities we have been in, and Ken was a little scared to risk it, tho there was no real danger, I think. We pulled out of the harbor shortly after noon, and got under way for Foochow.

June 13, 1922

Early Friday morning we entered the mouth of the Min River, and sailed up the beautiful Min valley until we reached Pagoda anchorage about 10 oclock. It was a ride I wouldnt have missed for a lot. The hills on both sides of the river are splendid terraced hills like the hills on the Rhine, except that instead of seeing castles every little ways, we would pass tall pagodas, old temples and little clustered fishing villages. The river was dotted with the sails of junks and sampans, big and little. I got my first glimpse of the big Ningpo junks employed in the coasting trade, with their peculiar shaped prow, and the great eyes staring so ferociously from each side. They are very impressive looking hulks, and very picturesque.

We took the launch from Pagoda anchorage up to Foochow city, and went to the home of the Munsens, the Y secretary here. That afternoon I had quite a long talk with Eva Melby, a Wisconsin girl who has just been out nine months, and then had a dandy game of tennis with some of the young fellows teaching in the Anglo-Chinese Middle School, and went over to Miss Melbys for dinner, where I met some more of the people, and had a mighty good time.

Saturday we went thru several very interesting schools, particularly the Anglo-Chinese College and the Anglican School, and about four oclock went on to a picnic with about thirty of the younger missionaries - The Anti Cob Web Club, as they call themselves, - and had one of the finest times I have had since I have been out here, getting home about midnight. If the people at home could have seen that bunch out for a good time, and could have heard the college and popular songs that we sang all the way back on the launch, I think they might revise their ideas of missionaries somewhat. It surely was a great bunch of young people, and we had our picnic up on a beautiful big hill at the foot of Kushan, a fine old mountain back of Fukien University.

Sunday we went over into the walled city, and went to church at the Congregational church, where we heard a handsome Chinese minister preach a sermon which we of course couldnt understand, but which Mr. MacConnell translated for us, and then we looked thru the Foochow College, which is the American Board Middle School. It is a mighty fine school. We had dinner with the MacConnells, and then went out to a school for blind boys that was most interesting, and to several other places of interest, including the old North Gate Tower, where one can get a splendid view of the whole city of Foochow, and in the other direction can look down on a vast stretch of rice paddies, cut by winding silver canals, and extending as far as the foot of the mountains. Foochow is located on a great island in the river, of which it occupies only a very small portion at one end. In spite of their immense population, these Chinese cities are small in area, because of the crowding. Foochow is a city of probably half a million, but it is not large at all. The basin in which it is located is completely surrounded by a ring of tall green covered mountains, which makes it one of the prettiest cities I have ever seen. It is wonderfully prosperous country, and one never sees more than a very few beggars. It is rather wild country, too, and there are maneating tigers within twenty or thirty miles of the city. One of the most famous tigers in the world, the "Blue Tiger," has terrorized a certain village for years, and no one has been able to get him. Roy Chapman Andrews conducted a special hunt for him when he was out here a few years ago, but he was unsuccessful. One of the missionaries at Yenping is a great hunter, and the A.C. Middle School has one of the tigers that he shot. There are also wild boars, and all sorts of smaller game in these mountains, too.

We came back to the south side of the river Sunday evening to the Munsens again, across the famous old stone bridge that they call the "Bridge of a Thousand Ages" and were certainly ready for bed after a mighty full day.

Monday we went down the river a mile or two to the Fukien Christian University, and spent the morning looking around their mighty fine little plant. They have just moved from the city, and many of their buildings are temporary, but they have a wonderful site on the side of the hill overlooking the Min, and they are beginning to put up some very fine buildings.

In the afternoon we climbed Kushan, the fine old peak I spoke of. Ken didnt feel that he was quite equal to the trip, so he went up in a chair, and Mr. Neff and I walked. It was a splendid climb of a couple of thousand feet, up to a big Buddhist Monastery. Unlike most of them, it is a really live monastery, and has a great many monks, and is immensely wealthly. The abbott is a member of the YMCA! That proves that he is a wide awake man, and his monastery shows it. It is very much like what one reads of the medieval monasteries, except that of course there are big Buddhas and little Buddhas, and laughing Buddhas and reclining Buddhas scattered all around the place. There were some funny things. They are vegetarians, and will not kill any animal, and in order to show their respect for life, they have a stable for old pigs and chickens and cows that the farmers bring in. They simply take good care of them until they die. However, they have nothing of the sort for people. They are performing no service at all for any human being, not even keeping an old folks home. Animals they feel they should care for, but the human animal can look out for itself.

We also saw some of the monks at their evening worship, which seemed rather cheap and not very impressive. It is not an inspiring thing to watch men worship idols, even tho they may some of them really be worshipping what the idol represents, and not the idol itself.

The trip up and down the mountain I wont soon forget. We went up a little rocky path, which wound up and up, thru little rice paddies and potato fields, where men and women were working away, barefooted and with their great broad hats, some of them plowing with these pretty little hill cattle to pull the plow - others weeding the rice, and others hoeing the potatoes with great crude hoes. As we got higher, the whole Foochow basin lay in a panorama below us - the long island, with a silver strip of river on each side - the bevy of dusky winged junks coming upriver on the incoming tide - the little clustered villages scattered over the plain, with a few wisps of smoke hanging over each one - the clean little rice paddies, cut here and there with little threadlike canals - and off to the right, the close-packed city of Foochow, with a crowd of anchored junks at the river bank. Frame all this flat basin with an irregular ring of mountains, extending range behind range as far as you can see, and hang a wine-red sun just over the western-most range, so that it lights up the clouds, and the mountains with a strong tinge of red, and you have some faint idea of the view that we had from old Kushan. Then and there we decided that Foochow was the prettiest city we have seen.

The mountain path was lovely, too. There were great wild mountain lilies in bloom, pure white, and larger than any Easter lily I have ever seen, and there were little shrubs with a pretty pink blossom, and there were jasmine blossoms that were more fragrant than the finest rose - Oh, it was great, believe me.

We came down and had dinner with the Bemans, and shortly thereafter caught our launch which brought us down to Pagoda to the good ship Ningshin, where we slept on board, and which is now plowing the salty brine of the China Sea as we wend our way northward, homeward, and Shanghaiward. And Thursday morning we ought to get to Shanghai and find some mail. OH BOY! It has been over <u>five weeks</u> since I have had a word from home.

June 20, 1922, Tuesday

These few days in Shanghai have surely been pretty full, even though it is the second time I have seen the city. There is always more to see here, it seems. The first couple of days were mostly full of business and necessary purchasing of a few articles of clothing and luggage. Then Saturday afternoon we went out to the Shanghai Baptist College to see their commencement exercises. It was very worth while attending. They gave prizes to the ones who had made the best record in each department, and there were a fine looking bunch of fellows that took them. It is very surprising to find how young higher education is in China. This college, one of the older and one of the best in China, only has 100 alumni. When you think how rapidly the number of graduates will multiply in the next few years, it is easy to see that there will be some great changes with these young well trained leaders coming into the management of things. In the evening we went to the alumni banquet, where I only escaped having to speak by the longwindedness of the fellow ahead of me.

Sunday morning we attended the big North Gate institutional church, a Southern Baptist church which is entirely independent of missionary control or support. I later learned at the home of Miss Kelly, the missionary who has been working in the church for the last twentyeight years, that the growth of the church in the last few years, and almost all of the institutional features, are due to the suggestions and work of Mr. Geldhart. That makes another fine bit of work to mark up to his credit.

Sunday afternoon we went out to Tung Wen college, the Japanese college, which I mentioned when I was in Shanghai before. Geldhart had set up a small conference for planning the work for next year. It is a very small association, very weak, in numbers at least, and working against strong opposition in the school. It was very interesting to see the boys really get inspired to the bigness of the job, and the opportunities ahead of them, as the meeting progressed. We had a very poor supper of supposedly Chinese food, in courtesy to the Chinese students from other colleges who had been invited in to help make the plans. The conference lasted until 9:30 and we got back about 10:30. The Chinese food rather had a riot most of the night, but the morning news reported everything quiet except for a few skirmishes.

Yesterday afternoon I went thru the factory of the Commercial Press, one of the oldest and best established Chinese firms in the city. They started in twentyfive years ago as a printing establishment, and have branched out into a great number of other things, until now their factory seems to turn out a most conglomerated assortment of things. They make books, print posters, labels, make postcards, etc. All the printing and lithographing is done on very modern machinery, a great deal of which they have manufactured themselves. There are no patent laws in China, so that they buy one foreign machine, and then make more if they need them. They manufacture all sorts of wooden and paper mache (?) toys, and various other things. There machinery department turns out all sorts of scientific appartus for schools, printing presses, and even a Chinese typewriter. The last is very interesting. It has three thousand characters, and is built on quite a different principle from our typewriters. It does not pay to use it to write just one letter, for you can write as fast by hand, but it is used for making duplicate letters. It is very compact, and doesnt take up much more room than a standard machine.

Not only was the factory interesting as a manufactory for so many different things, and as an example of what Chinese business men are capable of, but it was also extremely interesting in regard to labor conditions. You didnt need spectacles to see that the labor conditions were excellent. All the workers were happy looking and the girls and boys were all over twelve or fourteen, I should judge, and looked as well dressed as school children. However I was surprised to learn that they have a nine hour day. I didnt think anything but a twelve hour day existed in China. The men are given a bonus once a year, depending on their length of service in the company. The company maintains a savings department to help them to save their wages, and also a night school for the workers, and a day school for the children of the men. They have a maternity allowance, and even an old age pension. I doubt whether one could find much better conditions even in America. It was certainly great.

Today Mr. Hayes took a small party thru a silk filature. I found out he was planning to do it, so I attached myself to the party. I certainly am glad I did, for two reasons. In the first place, the processes were about as interesting mechanical processes as I have ever watched. First the cocoons are sorted as to size and grade by women and children. They they are put in very hot water to loosen the threads, and little girls swish them around with a brush until they get together the ends of the threads of a big bunch of cocoons. They hand them to the spinners who put them in a basin of hot water before them, and fasten the filaments of four to six cocoons to a whirling reel that simply unwinds the whole cocoon. It is fascinating to watch. Each cocoon has from five to seven hundred <u>yards</u> of filament. After it is wound on these reels it is dried and taken to the next room where some of it is unreeled for a test sample, and the skein is twisted and packed for shipment. They simply ship the skeins of filament, because there is a duty in the U.S. on thread. The thread is spun in New York. The biggest part of the work, and the most interesting is the great room where the women and children unwind the cocoons and that brings me to the second thing of interest. There are 300 girls and seven hundred women. All of them have to work right over steaming water all day long, and of course their hands are red and raw from the work, and their complexions have all the color steamed out of them. The little girls have to stand all day, though the spinners can sit down. Some of those girls are unbelievably small, and Mr. Hayes, who speaks Chinese, asked the foreman how old the youngest ones were. He said eight years, Chinese count, which means <u>six</u> or <u>seven</u> our count. Can you imagine that. Anyone who could see those tiny little kids (some of the poor little tykes were just having their feet bound and stood first on one foot and then on the other to ease the pain) - anyone who could see those little kids, and say that such things were all right, is not a Christian, by my definition. I dont care whether he believes the whole Bible from beginning to end or whether he believes every orthodox doctrine that ever was - I wouldnt call him a Christian. Those kids come to work at four thirty in the morning, and go home at quarter to eight at night. That isnt a guess - the manager himself told us that. They have an hour off at noon to eat their lunch in the factory - no place to go - no provision for any sort of recreation during that time, or what is more needed, a place for rest. Think of kids seven years old working fourteen hours and a quarter every day! I don't know how it makes other people feel, but it makes me see red, and wish I had a gun. I no longer wonder that people turn Bolshevik. I consider it mighty fortunate that I have all my life seen the other side of the question, for even with that it sometimes seems as if the best thing to do were to send the whole —— system to ——, where it came from. I'll admit that this morning, after I had seen the place, I filled in the above blanks with no uncertain words.

I wish I had thought to ask how often they had a day off, but from what I have seen of these factories, I suppose that they certainly didnt have more than one day in fourteen free. Two thousand women and kiddies, working fourteen hours day after day, over half of them bending over water that is almost boiling, in a room that must be as hot as the Black Hole of Calcutta on a really hot day - doing that for the munificent sum of from 20 to 50 cents Mex a day, or 12 to 30 cents gold. Somehow, silk will never look quite the same to me, I'm afraid. It has lost considerable of its luster.

Of course, one has got to look at the thing sanely. We may wish we could send the whole blankety-blank system to Hades in one fell swoop, but the fact remains that we cant. I had a long talk with Mr. Tchou, head of the industrial department of the Y yesterday. (Now that I've seen this silk filature, I think that I'll go up and see him agian.) He is really very sane and conservative himself, considering what he has seen, and takes this attitude, namely, that China simply cannot hope to avoid the terrible industrial history of England and America, but that what took a century and a half in England, and several generations in America, may take only decades in China. From the way the Chinese are learning to organize, I expect that he may be right. The Christian forces have a wonderful opportunity and a tremendous obligation to keep close to the labor movement here. There is no question that its theoretical aim is entirely Christian, and it is our duty to see that it is as nearly as possible always Christian in practice. It will be a terrible calamity if the church outlaws the labor movement from itself as it did in England, and to almost as large an extent in America. That policy has given a movement which is essentially Christian in its aim, over to leaders who are often not only men of low ideals, but who are in the game for their own personal gain. We have a chance here to keep its ideals high. Many of the men who are organizing some of the best unions here are Christians, as would be expected.

These labor upheavals here make me think of what the Korean missionaries said - "Why no, we didnt instigate any rebellion against Japan. We simply taught Christianity, and it is impossible for Christianity and tyranny to exist side by side." The missionaries here have done nothing, either, but lay down Christian principles - the Chinese are seeing to getting them put into practice as far as possible.

June 30, 1922. Friday

It has been some little time since I wrote up this voluminous volume, so I will have to just sketch in many of the things that have happened in the interval. Last Thursday night I got on board a river boat and started for Nantunchow. I got there the next noon as the boat was late, and after a few rather amusing incidents due to my somewhat sketchy knowledge of this language, I found the Christian Mission school, the only mission work here. They took me in like a long lost friend, tho I didnt know a one of them, and Dr. Garrett took me around the city. It is an interesting city because it is practically all the work of one man, Chang Chien. He is a very wealthy man who decided many years ago that he would make Nantunchow a model city in every way. So he built schools and good roads and some modern buildings, and the work has been going on ever since, so that now in places you would think that you were in an American city. Of course there is also the old Chinese city which can never be changed except by fire or dynamite, but the new city is fine and clean and prosperous looking. There are many factories in the city, but due to the lateness of my boat, we didnt have time to get around and see them. We did see the model jail, where all the prisoners are taught a trade, and a school for the blind and a school for the deaf and dumb. In America those might not be a curiosity, but as far as I know those are the only two schools of the sort in China which are not under mission auspices. Even here, when Chang Chien founded them he had to get Christian teachers, for no one else was trained for that work. In doing that he had to go against his one of his two pet ideas - that there shall be no foreign influence in Tungchow, and no Christian influence. Of course he doesnt use any coercion to exclude either, but he is very anxious that the city be a product of pure Chinese energy.

The most interesting thing we saw, however, was the big pagoda on Langshan. (shan means mountain. Incidentally this shan is the one Langshan chickens are named for.) The mountain, or rather the steep hill, for that is all it is, juts up out of the level alluvial plain of the Yangtse, like a wart on the back of your hand. From the top of the pagoda the sight is great. The fields are all very fertile, and the country supports an immense population, as can be seen from the little hamlets and villages scattered all over the plain. Cotton, rice, and wheat fields are placed side by side as far as you can see.

In the evening the young ladies of the mission, Mr. Otto, a young instructor and myself went to the Chinese theater. I have been anxious to go ever since I have been over here, and I surely was glad I went. The show lasts from six until midnight, but we went only form ten until midnight, as the things we wanted to see came at that time. First they had a "modern" play. They have tried to copy the western play, but if this was any sample, they have done very poorly. It was very poorly acted, and not at all finished, and was simply a cheap melodrama play. When the curtain went down on the last act, the orchestra started up. A Chinese orchestra is an inevitable accompaniment to any of the old plays. It is made up of about nine tenths drums and tom-toms, and one tenth squeaky Chinese fiddles and flutes. Aside from that, however, the play was great. The costumes were simply gorgeous, and the interest depended not so much on the plot as on the grace of the actors, the beautiful dances, and the splendid costuming. All the actors were men, even those who had womens parts, and they said that the main actor was one of the best in China, and I have no reason to doubt it. He ended up with a spirit dance that I dont think I will ever forget.

The audience was as interesting as the play. All classes and degrees of people were there from riksha coolies to Chang Chiens brother's wife. You are served tea while the show is going on, and everyone talks just as loud as they please, so that many times the actor is entirely drowned out.

The next morning I took the boat on up the river, and arrived at Nanking early Sunday morning. I again had some interesting experiences finding Rays house in a nasty drizzling rain, but finally got there and had breakfast. We had a good time Sunday and saw some parts of the city that I hadnt seen before, in spite of the rain.

Monday morning I went down to Hsiakwan, which is the real river port of Nanking, the city itself being located some miles back from the river. I wanted to see the work that Mr. Magee was doing there, having heard about it from Ken. There really wasnt a great deal to see, but Magee is doing the only Christian work that is being done in that dirty hell-hole mushroom port city. He has started a small institutional church, and expects to build a new church soon.

In the afternoon we did what I had been wanting to do for a long time. We went out with old Dr. Macklin to see some real country mission work, about 45 li out of town. We drove out in an old one horse cab, and had to get out and help the poor horse pull it up the hills, and finally reached our destination, a little filthy village, with one village street, where pedestrians, and little burros with great loads, and mangy dogs, and the ever-present black pigs, all competed for the right of way. We went into the tea house, and ordered tea, which tasted very good after our long ride. Then Dr. Macklin got out a bunch of pamphlets and tracts which he had brought along, and laid them on the table. Of course there was already a crowd around us, but that increased the crowd, and many of them came up and took copies of the literature. Dr. Macklin talked to them too, not in any preachy way, but just conversationally, and reducing his remarks to a level that they could understand. They were a most interesting crowd. I have never seen, I think, faces that showed so plainly the results of an animal existence. Stupid, hard faces, without a trace of anything higher than an animal spirit. They were all gamblers, just as all the lower class Chinese are gamblers, both men and women, and Dr. Macklin talked quite a little about that. They enjoyed it all and probably got some good out of it. It is just the leaven of that sort that has finally made Christianity a religion that is at least known by reputation all thru China. Then we left the tea house and went to the little village school, where one of the two Christians in the village is voluntarily, without pay, conducting a little boys primary school in his own house, which, tho dirty, is at least better than most. It was worth a dollar to see his face and the face of his wife. It is an astonishing fact that out here, almost two thirds of the time, you can tell a Christian simply by looking at his face. It makes a real difference in their whole lives, and it simply shows up unmistakably in their faces. Then too, Christianity is the only religion that stands for unselfish service to the community such as that man was rendering. It was great to get a chance to see what the work was like out here on the firing line. Dr. Macklin has twenty such villages under his charge, all within twenty miles of Nanking. Wednesday morning the 28th I came down to Soochow by train. Soochow I found almost as good as it had been described to me, in spite of the rain, which was almost incessant all the time I was there. It is an old city, with narrow streets that wind and twist in a way that is simply awful, and with a great many small canals cutting the city this way and that, always crowded with sampans and craft of all kinds. The bridges over the canals are almost all of the "camel back" variety, which sometimes makes it necessary to get out of your riksha and walk over the steps while the riksha man pulls the riksha up the steps bumpety-bumpety-bump, and down the other side, bumpety-bumpety-bump.

    I spent quite a little time at the fine new YMCA with Mr. Geldhart, but did as much sightseeing as the rain would permit. We went to the big Buddhist city temple, which had nothing unusual about it except that it was actually being used as a place of worship, which is not at all true of most of them. The priests were talking to a group of people in the temple, expounding some of their beliefs, an entirely new thing for Buddhism, and due of course to the effect of Christianity. Another thing we saw was the plendid big nine story pagoda, one of the largest I have seen anywhere. From the top a fine view of the city is obtained, and one can see six of the seven pagodas of this "city of Seven Pagodas."

July 4, 1922

I left Soochow early Friday morning for Shanghai, and met Mr. Geldhart when he came thru on the same train the next morning and we proceeded together to Mokanshan. We left the train at Hangchow, and took a small launch up the famous old Grand Canal, which has its southern end at Hangchow, and which was originally built to carry the tribute rice from these provinces to Peking. Boats of all descriptions ply up and down its broad muddy way, some of them going along under sail, some being rowed, some being towed, and some a combination of all three methods. Those that had to tow their craft were in hard straits, for the water was at flood, and the tow paths along the side were from two to three feet under water, so that they had to wade along pulling their heavy boats. Another interesting type of craft are the small "foot-boats." They are simply small sampans, rowed by a man sitting in the stern, who rows with his <u>feet</u>. They are very common all thru this part of the country.

After a few miles on the Grand Canal, we branched off into one of the smaller canals which form a network all thru the alluvial plain, and by evening we arrived at the little village nearest to the foot of Mokanshan. Some of the people with us took chairs, but Mr. Geldhart and I preferred to walk. It was four miles across a muddy plain, and then four miles up a good road to the houses which are perched on the very peak of the mountain. As it was raining pretty hard all the way up, we were a sight for sore eyes when Mrs. Geldart finally let us in the door at 10:30 that night. There was a hot supper for us, tho, and a hot bath, and a good bed, so that our troubles for that day were ended.

I forgot to mention that at one place where our launch couldnt get thru one big bridge on account of the high water, and we had to walk a mile or so up to another launch, we met Emory Luccock on a house boat and he went the rest of the way with us on the launch.

I have met many fine people here, and have had a good time with the Geldart kids. Had several long talks with Luccock, and heard him make the Fourth of July address today.

July 10, 1922

The night of the Fourth five of us who were anxious to get to Hangchow decided to risk taking a houseboat, tho the launch service had been discontinued on account of the high water. We piled into a little dinky boat that night after a fine walk down the mountain on a fairly moonlight night, much better than our walk up it the first night. I was tired enough after that eight mile walk on top of the walking we had done during the day to sleep even on the soft pine boards which were provided for the purpose. I woke up when the old boatman was shouting directions to his other man, just before we shot thru the bridge where the water was highest, but it wasnt nearly as bad as it had been on the way up. That was about four in the morning, and after a not very exciting morning cramped up in our little boat we reached the railway station a little after noon and got to Hangchow College about three oclock.

The conference was most interesting from several points of view. In the first place it was the first YM conference here in China to be made up entirely of college men. There were no middle school students at all among the hundred men there. That of course raised the level of the conference considerably. Then it was interesting to me because I met again so many of the men that I have met all over this part of China, both foreigners and Chinese. The only drawback to the whole conference was that I had to speak twice - one very short talk, and one longer one.

One of the two afternoons I was there we went in to the city of Hangchow to do a little sightseeing adn shopping. It was raining as usual, so that I am afraid that I was not properly impressed by the beauty of the city, which is supposed to be one of the most beautiful in China. They do have some fine old pagodas scattered around in strategic points. The College itself has a beautiful location right on the hills on the bank of a fairly large river, which reminds me a great deal of the Min at Foochow. Just a short distance from the college is a big twelve story pagoda right beside the river, which is unusual as they are usually located as high as possible. However I found out that this particular pagoda was put up to keep away the evil spirits at this point in the river, which used to be very dangerous. The course or the nature of the river has changed long since, and it is simply a placid stream at that point, but still the majestic old pagoda is keeping its watch against the evil spirits.

It was very hard to break away from the conference to come to Shanghai to get my boat. It seemed almost like going away from home to leave so many friends behind, many of whom I may never see again. Egbert Hayes, John Geldart, Gale and Mrs. Seaman, little Mr. Tai, Tom Wong, and all the rest, a mighty choice bunch, and men with whom I have formed mighty close friendships even tho I have only been with them a short time, comparatively speaking. They were certainly kind enough in what they said about me when they told me good bye. It is an awfully pleasant experience to have men whom you admire and like speak highly of what you have tried to do, even tho you may know that you dont deserve any of what they are saying. I guess though that I wouldnt have any trouble getting a job out here, at any rate, tho these men want me to finish my school work first before they start offering me anything definite, as Mr. Paul of India did at the Conference. He promised me a job right now on the student YM staff if I would come out to India immediately. However the more I see out here, the more the importance of the best education I can get grows on me, so that there is no temptation to accept such offers.

I left Hangchow Friday noon and got to Shanghai that night. Saturday was a hectic and busy day, trying to round up all the odds and ends that have to be finished before one sails. Saturday night Paul Cressey arrived from Swatow, and as Miss Boss from Chaochaofu was already at the Missionary Home, we had a good talk fest, expecially Paul and I. He is going up to Mokanshan for the summer.

Sunday afternoon he escorted me down to the tender at the Customs Jetty, and in crossing the little gang plank onto the tender I took my feet off Chinese soil for at least some time to come. I cant make myself believe that I have taken them off of Chinese soil forever. I surely hated to leave. There is something about China that "gets" you. I dont know what is is - it is a combination of so many things, I think, that is is hopeless to try and define it, but get you it does, whether you can define it or not. I think that I felt a good deal more blue pulling out of Woosung harbor on this old ship, the China, than I did pulling out of Frisco harbor on the old Taiyo.

I should like to sort of sum up my impressions of China, but I find that that is utterly impossible. To try to give your impressions of an experience extending over four months which has changed your whole outlook on many questions economic, political, international, and religious, an experience that is continually going to have a deeper effect on your life the further you get from it, is quite impossible for me. It surely has been the greatest, and perhaps will always be the greatest experience of my life. That kind of an experience it is rather difficult to describe.

There are several fine young Chinese students on board going to America, one of whom I met in Foochow, and several others that I have gotten acquainted with here on board, who will keep the trip to Yokohama from being boresome on this old tub. Then after what will undoubtably a short eight days in Japan, we, that is Ken and I, strike for home, and perhaps for some place besides home, too. Yea Bo!

July 17, 1922

I am now in Tokyo, but I will go back and tell about our day at Nagasaki on the way here. We stopped at Nagasaki early the morning of the 11th, and most of us went on shore about ten oclock. I went with about eight Chinese students on their way to America, and did what I could to help them have a good time. There wasnt a great deal in the city that interested me, for I had seen Japanese cities before, but we went to a nice old Shinto shrine, and to a few other "Places of interest." We had lunch at a Chinese restaurant, for these poor Chinese boys were just starving for a bite of good home food. I have had the time of my life helping them translate the menus into language that they can understand. Naturally, they arent keen about foreign food as yet.

The most interesting thing by far though, at Nagasaki, was to watch them coaling our ship. This is the famous port where ships are coaled by women. As soon as we had cast anchor in the harbor, large barges loaded with coal drew up alongside and the men and women on board the barges began constructing a crude sort of stairway, or series of platforms, up the side of the ship. Then the real work began. They pass the coal up those stairways in little baskets which hold I suppose from 20-25 pounds of coal, and the baskets move along the line almost as fast and as regularly as if it were a machine conveyor. It is astonishing to see how fast they can pass the baskets up to the women above them without hardly ever spilling one, or having to wait for her to take it. In the late afternoon when they were going their best trying to get thru before dark, I timed them and found that on one line probably forty people long, reaching from the far end of the large barge up to the ship, and then thirty feet up the ships side, they were passing fifty five baskets to the minute, almost one per second. Believe me, that means fast work.

If you want to know what people mean by a "sense of social guilt" I think you ought to stand as I did for a couple of hours and watch those women slave away in the blazing sun, grimy and dirty, without a chance to rest even for a moment, and then meditate on the fact that <u>you</u> are partly responsible for those conditions. Those women are submitting to those conditions, and slaving their lives out, simply to get <u>you</u> across the ocean, and yet <u>you</u> go calmly ahead and let them do it, without a thought for anything but your own comfort. That to my mind, is a good example of the fact that we are each one of us responsible to a certain extent for the unchristian conditions that we find around us.

Stairway to Shinto shrine

Here at Tokyo I have spent quite a little of my time sightseeing. I have seen the Osakusa Temple where there is a wooden Buddha rubbed into an almost shapeless lump by people who are suffering pain, and who believe that if they have a sore eye, for instance, they can cure it by rubbing the eye of the Buddha and then rubbing their own eye. It was a terribly cheap and tawdry looking place.

Then I spent most of Saturday out at the Tokyo Peace Exposition, which is a great industrial exposition of everything made in Japan. It is simply astonishing to see the range and variety of things that are being manufactured. I think that there are very few things that we make in the States, that are not being made out here, though I also doubt whether they ever make any really first class, A #1 things. They have a bad reputation for making things that are "just as good."

Then yesterday afternoon with Mr. Kobashi again, I went out to the Meiji shrines, a beautiful big Shinto shrine, only completed a few years ago, to the memory of the Meiji, one of the best of the Japanese emperors. These Japanese certainly know how to locate their temples. I dont think that their temples are as impressive as those of China, but they nearly always locate them in a grove of trees, and manage to give them a much more beautiful surrounding than one finds in China. This shrine is in a grove of tall cedar trees, in the middle of an immense park, and the buildings are all built in a very simply style of architecture, out of plain unpainted wood, which is well polished to show the grain. I think there was more of an atmosphere of worship lingering around those great wooden pillars than in any temple I have seen except the Temple of Heaven in Peking.

Meridian Day, 1922

This is the first day that I have ever lived that has had no date. It is located between July 26 and 27, and we are up near the Aleutian Islands, about four days out of Yokohama, homeward bound on the Empress of Asia. I will go back and pick up the thread of my discourse where I broke off, however.

View of Mt. Fuji from a distance

Ever since we came out, I have sort of had a hankering to climb Mt. Fuji, and Ken and I even got so far as planning to do it, but he isnt feeling well enough yet to do anything of that strenuous sort, so that I realized that it was up to me if I was going to get up the old mountain at all. Consequently, I decided to start down to Gotemba, the town nearest the foot, and see whether I couldnt find someone to climb with me, because I was not at all anxious to climb alone, not knowing a word of Japanese. Luck was with me, and I picked up two nice chaps at the Japan Tourist Bureau, one a Scotchman and the other an Australian, who were planning to make the climb, so we went together. When we got to Gotemba, we would have been utterly out of luck, not knowing the language, if it had not been for the fact that I knew that there was a missionary summer community nearby and we found the way to that. There the people fixed us up with lunches, advice, and some extra clothing, and we started out in a car to Subashiri, the little village where the beginning

MY TRIP TO CHINA

Resting 12,365 feet above the sea

Almost at the summit: Carl in the center of the right-hand photograph
(Handwriting is that of Howard Kirschenbaum)

The flag at the summit.

Flag at the summit: "I wish you could have heard the shout that came from the many pilgrims at various stages of the climb, when the sun finally shoved its white-hot brim up thru those soft white clouds."
(Handwriting is that of Howard Kirschenbaum)

of the climb is made. We started from there about five thirty in the afternoon and went up thru the woods in the most pitchblack darkness that I ever want to see. We had no lantern and simply followed our guide, stumbling along the path, always "backsliding" in these lava cinders, which make the walking just about like a path of deep sand.

    About nine or nine thirty we got above the timber line, and from there on the trip was wonderful. All the clouds and mist had cleared away, and the stars seemed so close you could almost reach up and touch them. I have never seen so many stars with my naked eye. It looked as if you were looking thru a telescope. We stopped every now and then at the rest houses along the way, and about ten thirty stopped for a meal, and laid down to sleep until one oclock. However, our plans were interrupted, for a little before twelve Weir had an awful chill, and we had to take some strenuous measures to keep him from cramping up so that we couldn't untie the knot. We decided he hadnt ought to lay down again so we started on again. The climb was getting steeper and steeper, and the rarity of the air was beginning to bother the other two fellows, and we were very tired, and the guide peeved because we hadnt let him sleep until one oclock, etc, etc, so that traveling for the next few hours was far from pleasant, in spite of the beautiful sky. A slender silver crescent of moon began to show up about twelve thirty, adding to the light of the stars, and making our pathway considerably plainer. At three oclock we stopped again at the sixth of the nine stations. Phelps had told me that we should be at the eighth station by four oclock if we wanted to see the sunrise from the top, so that at three thirty, I got the bunch started again, but their pace was entirely too slow. I wanted to get to the top, so I took a few sandwiches from the pack that the guide was carrying, and started out at my own pace. It was very cold now,

MY TRIP TO CHINA

and we had to keep moving to keep the sweat from freezing. The east was just beginning to show a few streaks of light, and I knew that I would have to hurry. When I was just a little above the eighth station, the view in the east became so wonderful that I watched it for some time. The country around the foot of the mountain, as far as one could see in every direction, was covered with a thick blanket of billowing white clouds, looking for all the world like a great expanse of foaming ocean breakers, frozen silent in mid-air. On the eastern edge of this expanse, there was a great glowing light coming up from beneath that colored the sky all colors of the rainbow. There was a perfect prismatic scheme of colors, blue, fading into purple, green yellow and red. It was one of the most beautiful sights I have ever seen, looking across that snowfield of clouds. In a little while the light became stronger and stronger, the clouds began to be tinged with pink - then the light becomes brilliant, and more brilliant, and then - Hurrah! the SUN. I wish you could have heard the shout that came from the many pilgrims at various stages of the climb, when the sun finally shoved its white-hot brim up thru those soft white clouds. And I shouted too, and waved my cap. We had seen a tremendous event.

I got to the top about six oclock, and the others about two hours later. As the clouds cleared away, it was a tremendous panorama that was spread out before us, great hills, and rivers and villages, and the sea, a wonderful sight, and little clouds drifting far above the hills, yet far, far below your feet - somehow there is a great new sensation just to be that far above the world at large.

I walked around the crater - filled with snow now, but two miles or more in circumference, and then about nine thirty we started down, and by three oclock were taking our baths at the little Ninooka Club from which we started. That evening we had a wonderful view of old Fuji, unobstructed by hardly a cloud. She looks much more wonderful, after one has climbed the 12,365 feet that separates her peak from the level of the sea.

July 30, 1922

Unless something very exciting happens between here and home, I think that this entry will end the journal, except that after I get home I will try and find time to put in one more entry, giving my reactions on getting home.

It has been a very smooth trip across, which is very unusual on this northern route, even at this time of year. Although I havent accomplished so very much that can be seen, yet the trip has been one of the most productive weeks that I have spent away from home. In the first place, I have been thinking over, talking over, and meditating over my experiences and impressions of China and the East. That has been valuable. Then in the second place, I have been putting in a great deal of time thinking about what part I shall take, and what attitude I shall take toward the Y work at school next fall. Of one thing I am sure - namely, that about nine-tenths of our work looks utterly futile when one gets away and gets a chance to look at it from a distance. My main job when I get back, as I see it, is to get the men to think - and when I have gotten them to thinking a little bit, then to get them to think some more - and some more! Most of us have never thought our way thru to find out what the real purpose of a YM should be, and our work shows that we have never found what the purpose should be. So, as I told Ken, my main job when I get back will be to make men thoroly uncomfortable, to drag them out and make them think. And then incidentally, I have just three little things that I myself want to do - just three things, and if I can do them they will really count for something, but I'm not even telling now what they are.

Then the third thing I have been accomplishing on board this time, has been some mighty concentrated thinking for myself. I decided long before we started that I was going to get next to Dr. Sharman, and I have. I also decided that I would try to get some of his ideas on religious questions, and some of his methods of student work, and I have. What I didnt calculate was that he had also laid his wires for me, and that he would make me lose more than one night's sleep on this trip doing some of the deepest thinking I have ever done. He is the most stimulating man I have ever been with, and it has been a wonderful opportunity to be with him.

A changed man: Carl after his return to the U.S.

CALENDAR

This calendar is intended to provide an overview of where Carl traveled, the major activities in which he was involved, and some broad themes and meanings he was exploring. It provides a detailed overview of what the trip involved. After multiple reads, the process of constructing the calendar was helped by approaching the diary in a systematic, organizing yet phenomenological way. The calendar may provide the reader a quick reference for reading, re-reading, finding, or citing specific passages. It may provide a visual and/or chronological aid for those who process, learn, and grow by such means.

In most instances, location, events, and themes were made with minimal inference, to encourage "empathy" for Carl and avoid "interpretation" of what was in many ways a personal exploration. Carl asserted and supported the notion that empathy is an under-appreciated and highly valuable way of understanding persons. He also believed that the "facts are friendly," that careful, systematic examination was important even as intuitive understanding was important. Carl proposed that the congruent, fully functioning person was extensional or concerned with multiple perspectives – objective, subjective, intersubjective, and particularly early and late in life, spiritual. Providing concrete information on locations and activities is accompanied by abstract information on topics or themes, but only at a broad level, encouraging idiosyncratic understandings in the reader. This broad approach to cataloging the diary also helps to provide consistency of organization given the variability of length, depth, and specificity that the diary provides.

The calendar identifies locations, activities and events that Carl described, in some cases in the actual words he used from the diary. Furthermore the calendar provides abstract themes or emotional topics. Attempts were made to use Carl's own words to describe the theme or topic, however, in some instances the theme was not directly named by Carl but appeared sufficiently related to warrant the reader's consideration. Themes and topics are intended to help the readers to begin an exploration of meaning, but are not intended as assertions of what Carl was "really" discussing, feeling or thinking about or what was "really" important in his experience or in the history, psychology, religion, or the development of ideas. In some cases location names, particularly in China, have changed, and are sometimes included in parentheses, but for space considerations and ease of reference to the diary, the names used by Rogers in 1922 are consistently the ones used in the calendar (e.g., Beijing was called Peking, Fuzhou was called Foochow). Entries were created by Jef Cornelius-White. For about half (52%) of the calendar entries, a graduate assistant, Keith Wilson, provided a second, independent reader, which rendered feedback for corroboration, or in a few instances, alteration, of the content of locations, events, and themes. The entries between March 26th and June 30th were the ones that were formed from two persons' opinions, which represent some of the most complicated classifications due to a higher proportion of narration of previous days and density of profound themes.

This final paragraph provides details on how Carl narrated earlier days within other days and how that is cataloged in the calendar. The calendar provides information about 110 days from 61 entries during his approximately 172-day trip. In 49 instances, marked with an *, calendar information is provided when Carl gave thorough descriptions of adjacent earlier days. Blank days reflect the absence of an entry or thorough description on the next entry. On March 5th, Carl described March 1st and 3rd. Carl wrote two entries for March 12th, the first describing March 10th and 11th, and the second describing March 12th. April 3rd represents one of the richest entries in the journal in terms of Carl's passion, the density of ideas and the number of days and people discussed. Accordingly calendar entries from March 29th to April 3rd include influences from the April 3rd diary entry. Carl gave individual entries for the week before April 10th within the April 10th entry. Like the entry on April 3rd, the entry on April 10th is immensely rich with information and ideas. The May 3rd entry describes travel adventures between April 29–May 2nd. May 11th narrates time back to May 5th and involves attendance at the National Chinese Y Conference, community speeches, and a reunion with the American delegation. The May 17th entry also describes May 15th and 16th, which involve conditions "honestly the worse I have ever seen" and contemplations about the extinction of humanity "within generations." On May 24th, again after days without an entry, he described events and thoughts back to May 19. June 7th describes two days prior in detail and are listed on the calendar. The June 13th entry includes information back to June 9th mostly in Foochow, and the June 20th entry includes information back to June 17th while he is in Shanghai. June 30th includes information on select days back to June 22nd, involving experiences in several Chinese cities. Carl labeled one day as Meridian Day, which for him took place between July 26th and 27th crossing the international dateline and is listed on July 27th, and which confirms his July 22nd departure home. Also in this entry, Carl described events of approximately

July 19th and 20th in which he climbs Mt. Fuji overnight in freezing conditions. During the climb, Carl is intermittently by himself and with other random travelers. The entry climaxes in experiencing the sunrise at the summit and hearing all of the pilgrims at different stages of the climb shouting for joy at brilliance of the pink emerging on the horizon.

CALENDAR

February 1922

SUN	MON	TUE	WED	THU	FRI	SAT
12	13	14	15 At home – Wheaton, IL Skating; Departing How the trip will change him; Religious belief in action	16 Iowa – Nebraska – Colorado Travel; Almost missed train Observing scenery; Cross-cultural communication	17 Wyoming – Utah Travel Enjoying scenery; Reality of trip setting in	18 California – San Francisco Train travel; Meets travelers Loving scenery; Preparing for interactions with cohort
19 San Francisco, Oakland, Berkeley, Claremont Attend church; Sightseeing "Psychic stuff"; Forms of Christianity; Enjoyment; Provincialism	20 Chinatown, Golden Gate, Presidio Visa; Sightseeing; Attend church; Meeting John Mott Solitude and communion	21 At sea Boarding ship; Meeting Y delegation; Rough waves Excitement of departure and sea travel; First impressions of his fellow travelers	22 At sea Interacting with Profs. King, LaTourette and others "Can't get enough of these talks"; "Really thinking"; Valuing wide experience	23 At sea Walking; First delegation meeting; Writing Growing admiration for Mott; Loving the ocean; Time management	24 At sea Walking; Talking; Writing; Reading; Meeting; Enjoying describing a day in the life at sea, "More fun than a box of monkeys"	25 At sea Thinking; Edit a playful delegation newsletter; Talk "Search our own lives & faith as never before"; Principles of brotherhood

181

February and March 1922

SUN	MON	TUE	WED	THU	FRI	SAT
26 At sea Attend church; Marathon discussion; Writing Spiritual life as exercise; What is a Christian?; Questioning	27 Honolulu Attend university; Sightseeing; Observe races Enjoy land and sea; Prizing the people of Hawaii	28	1* At sea Saw porpoises; Costume ball Cherishing life on boat	2	3* At sea Lost day due to date line "It is too deep and complicated for me"	4
5 At sea Discussion & weather; Rough seas "Hammering out our faith in the forge of discussion"	6	7	8 At sea Prizing cohort; Discussion of politics & religion Pacifism; Faith on an "unsearchable path"	9	10* Yokohama, Japan Meet officials, Landing; Ride rickshaws "He was a man, not an animal"; Visceral experience of Orient	11* Tokyo, Japan Sightseeing; Observing; Eating Indecency of human labor; Wonder at culture

CALENDAR

March 1922

SUN	MON	TUE	WED	THU	FRI	SAT
12	13	14	15	16	17	18
Tokyo Church with Japanese Parliament; Meeting delegates Dispelling pessimism; Making the most of life	Nikko and mountains Train travel; Shinto shrines Beauty and wonder of Japan; Finding God in oneself	Tokyo Sightsee and eat Appreciating language barriers and human connections to transcend	Countryside Train travel; Absorbed in scenery "New impressions!"; Prizing the land, its beauty and function	Kyoto See craftwork, shops, temples, university Gratitude for service, admiration of skill, beauty, and Japanese people	Kyoto – Nara See temples; Diabutsu Buddha Buddhism "appeals only to the ignorant"	Kobe Travel and reflect American influence, industrialization & exploitation of people, labor issue
19	20	21	22	23	24	25
Kobe Attend church; Write; Discuss "Whether war was ever justifiable"	Traveling; Sheminoseki Train & boat travel; Enjoying scenery "One grand panorama"	At sea – Fusan, Korea Traveling; Gaining impressions of Korea "A sad contrast"	Seoul Sightsee and shop; "Meet higher-ups of Korea" "Slipped out .... when no one was looking"; Oppression	Seoul Meet Korea Y and hear speech "We are sitting on a pent up volcano"; Japanese suppression	Seoul – Antung Reflecting; Discussing previous night; Traveling Christianity is a force to be feared by power; Self-sacrifice	Mukden – Manchuria, China Traveling; Mott and General Chang talk Inhumane animal treatment; Work and reflection

183

March and April 1922

SUN	MON	TUE	WED	THU	FRI	SAT
26	27	28	29	30*	31*	1*
Peking (Beijing) Church; Rikshaws; Dine with "ex-enemies"; Lectures "Taste of Peking"; The experience is like "a dream"	Peking (Beijing) Sightsee Forbidden City, Temple of Heaven "People are the real thing", "He is also a symptom of condition of the people"	Peking (Beijing) Visit Union Medical College; Attend 20-course dinner "Education of China"; "Chinese were fully the equals of the Americans"	Peking (Beijing) General Committee meets; Advocate for more student reps Surprise, obstacles, healthy discussion – commission formed to consider it	Peking (Beijing) Decide inclusion of movements and relief work "Simply necessary – not awfully interesting"	Peking (Beijing) Discuss attitudes towards persons of other faiths "Evening one of the most inspiring"; Christian capitalism and harm	Peking (Beijing) Reflecting on sessions "Quit theologizing and begin really practicing … then revolutionizing the world will really begin"
2*	3	4*	5*	6*	7*	8*
Peking (Beijing) Reflecting on developing "truly international mind" Differences yet	Peking (Beijing) Discuss international purpose and stance on war Despair, no agreement but	Peking (Beijing) Visit Tsing Hua College; Opening of conference with Mott speech "Laid out with	Peking (Beijing) Continue conference; Hiked to Summer Palace; Reception	To Great Wall Attend meetings; Travel to Great Wall Anti-Christianity critiques;	Peking (Beijing) Skip meeting for baseball Realization and pursuit of self-care needs	Peking (Beijing) Speak for American Delegation; Sub-committee meets

CALENDAR

April 1922

SUN	MON	TUE	WED	THUR	FRI	SAT
2 contd. importance of "one in Christ" and "undergrad in spirit"; "Days and people I will never forget"	3 contd. "unity of spirit"; Policy of nonviolence "The brink of new Christian Era"	4* contd. admirable taste just suited for a college campus", "good speech by Dr. Mott"	5* contd. International viewpoints, on "Social Industrial Problems" "The student and the church," and other	6* contd. "Superstition" v. "an intellectual basis"; Christianizing the social order	7*	8* contd. Not getting "anywhere" on war; Open disagreement with Ex-Chancellor of German Empire; Pacifism
9* Peking (Beijing) Committee meeting; Dine at the Smith's Questioning "A spiritual unity deeper than differences" or change through differences	10 Peking (Beijing) Reflecting on committee speakers, ideas, and personal growth "Live our Christianity," Being "wide awake": Critical, honest, brave and extensional	11	12	13	14 To Uet Hsu and Taiku Traveling; Describing land and soldiers; Visit hospital Interest in the lands and people in which he is traveling	15 Taiku – Uet Hsu – Taiyuanfu Speak at school; Jail house visit; Tour Girls' School "See real mission work outside of the cities"

185

April 1922

SUN	MON	TUE	WED	THUR	FRI	SAT
16 Taiyuanfu Lead Easter service; Dine with Model Governor Adding "to the illusion" of place	17 Taiyuanfu Speak to soldiers and boys; Indulge in feast Guilt over decadence	18 Shikiachuang Navigating train system; Writing "War, war, & rumors of war", pretty certain to come	19 Chengchow Tour industrial city "Not very inspiring" without student work	20	21 Chengchow Tour mill; Consider inhumane labor issues "We need" managers to see "Everyone of them with great possibilities"	22 Hankow Admire lush land; Talk with crowd "People are tremendously curious"; "It is hard to get used to being a foreigner"
23* Hankow Lead morning service at boys' school; Talk to crowd; Talk to Hankow Y Foreign Y Men: Princes among men	24 Hankow Elude pursuers	25* Hankow Visit Hanyang Iron Works	26 Hankow Visit Yangtze Engineering Works Imagine a "system more devilish"; International exploitation; Receptive students	27	28	*29 Hankow – Nanking Travel on river boat "Started off in a blaze of firecrackers," loved time on boat

CALENDAR

April and May 1922

SUN	MON	TUE	WED	THU	FRI	SAT
						*30
						To Nanking Lounge on boat "quiet"
*1	*2	*3	4	*5	*6	
Nanking Describe city; Visit South Gate & Temple of Confucius Admire immense city	Wuchang Visit University; Walk on Wall; Dine with Ray "Simply trying to defy change"	Wuchang Typing on train Reconciling images with that of home		Shanghai Attend National Christian Conference of China Time to "bind the work together"	Shanghai Continue conference with a thousand people "Fundamentals of faith"	
*7	*8	*9	*10	11	12	13
Shanghai Visit Girls' School; Visit Shanghai Baptist College; Consider gender & culture Doing a "heart good"	Shanghai Visit English School; Visit Japanese University A "stupid attitude"; "the finest piece of work"	Shanghai Listen to Chinese men & women's chorus Enjoy not such "serious pursuits"	Shanghai Welcome reunion with American delegation "Members of three races, but all Americans"	Shanghai to Manila Depart on boat "Waiting on the tide to come in"		
14	15*	16*	17	18	19*	20*
Island of Luzon, Philippines Boat docks;	Manila, Philippines Visit hospital;	Manila, Philippines Talk to Mr.	Manila, Philippines Talk to Judge, &		Hong Kong Tour city & hospitals	Hong Kong – Canton Meet with 20

187

May 1922

SUN	MON	TUE	WED	THU	FRI	SAT
14 contd. Attend young people's meeting Consider history	15 contd. Tour city and ruins; Sleep on boat Poverty, "honestly the worse I have ever seen"; Christian superstitions and decadence	16 contd. Corpus; Explore monastery; Travel country The veil is lifted: "life is just one long siesta"	17 contd. General Wood; Board boat Wonder if humanity will go extinct "within generations;" "I am always so lucky…. It means a big responsibility"	18	19 contd. "A typical port"	20 contd. Catholic fathers "interesting" mission work
21* Canton Go to Canton Christian College (CCC); Spend night at Mr. Lerigo's "Civic pride," 1911 Revolution remembrance	22* Canton Visit Hospital for the Insane; Learn about local government; Return to CCC Inhumane treatment leads to insanity; Political affairs "In a terrible	23* Canton Travel down river; Pay a "kumshaw" to the pirates; guard of turbaned Sikhs Valuing travel	24 Hong Kong Work, read, rest "I could make up quite a hair-raising story with typhoons, pirates, bandits, but since I am a little too truthful," we are quite safe	25	26	27 Hong Kong Read newspaper; Reflect on Chinese politics; Reflect on river life "A man who can reconcile both parties," and "unite China"; "The

May and June 1922

SUN	MON	TUE	WED	THUR	FRI	SAT
21	22 contd. muddle"; Doing "pioneer work" in agricultural education	23	24	25	26	27 contd. bareness of existence must be beyond comprehension"
28	29	30	31	1	2* Swatow (Shantou) Describing region; Visiting schools Appreciate school and community	3
4	5	6* Chowchowfu (Chaozhou) Sightsee Confucian & Baptist sites Democratic progress, Persevering &	7 Swatow; At sea Returning and departing Making friends; Concern with possible typhoon	8 At sea; Amoy (Xiamen) Relief of typhoon; Sightseeing on island "No real danger"	9* Min River to Pagoda to Foochow (Fuzhou) Impressive boat travel; Meet new people "A mighty good time"	10* Foochow (Fuzhou) Enjoy picnic Not your average missionary

CALENDAR

189

June 1922

SUN	MON	TUE	WED	THUR	FRI	SAT
4	5	6 contd. open-minded leadership	7	8	9	10
11* Foochow (Fuzhou) Attend church; Visit colleges; Sightsee a "wonderfully prosperous country"	12* Foochow (Fuzhou) Climb Kushan; Visit Buddhist monastery; Dinner with friends; Board boat. "The prettiest city" ever seen"	13 Pagado anchorage to Shanghai Reflecting while on board ship No mail for five weeks	14	15	16	17* Shanghai Shanghai Baptist College for commencement The future of education abroad
18* Shanghai Attend church; Visit college "Inspire to the bigness of the job"	19* Shanghai Tour factory of Commercial Press Good work conditions make for happy people	20 Shanghai Visit silk works Non-Christian values make for poor work	21	22* Nantunchow Visit mission school; See Chinese Theater Finding America in China	23	24

June and July 1922

SUN	MON	TUE	WED	THU	FRI	SAT
25* Nanking Find Ray's house Discover new in old	26* Hsiakwan See mission work A needle in a haystack	27	28* Soochow Time at YMCA; Sightsee Side "effect of Christianity"; Rickshaws, "Bumpety-bumpety-bump"	29	30 Soochow – Hangchow Reflect on past days "Voluminous volume"	1
2	3	4 Hangchow – Mokanshan village Travel by interesting boat and hiking; Climbed mountain Enjoyed long talks; "Decided to risk" adventure	5* Houseboat to Hangchow Attend first YM College Congress in China; Gave speeches; Visited pagodas "Like going away from home to leave so many friends behind"	6	7	8* Shanghai Getting ready to sail; Meeting friends

July 1922

SUN	MON	TUE	WED	THU	FRI	SAT
9* Woosung harbour Boarding boat "There is something about China that 'gets' you"	10 On board ship to Tokyo Catching up; Meeting Chinese students	11* Nagasaki Sightsee; Watch women coaling ships "a sense of social guilt"; "You are partly responsible for those conditions" "yet you let them do it"	12	13	14	15* Tokyo Visit Tokyo Peace Exposition Astonishing industrial exposition
16* Tokyo Visit Meiji shrines "An atmosphere of worship" at temple in woods	17 Tokyo Catching up	18	19* To Gotemba and Mt. Fuji Vividly describing climb overnight A big adventure; "I realized it was up to me"	20* Mt. Fuji Top of Mt. Fuji at sunrise "We had seen a tremendous event"; "A great new sensation"	21	22* Left Yokohama Depart "Homeward bound"

July 1922

SUN	MON	TUE	WED	THU	FRI	SAT
23	24	25	26	27 At sea near Aleutian Islands Remembering his Mt. Fuji experience Living on a day with no date	28	29
30 At Sea Thinking; Talking (especially with Sharman); Meditating My Main Job: "Get men to think"; Religion; Education	31					

PROMINENT THEMES IN THE DIARY

The "Calendar" identifies many of the times, locations, activities, and themes of the diary. This chapter reflects on some of the meanings identified in these themes. While readers will inevitably be drawn to the meanings that are of import from their own perspective and intent, this reflection highlights some of the most prominent themes for me [Jef]. I have tried to focus on the most frequently occurring themes and integrate them according to my own understanding of Carl as a 20-year-old, and to a lesser extent to the person-centered approach to therapy and beyond. There are four themes that stand out for me: (1) an existential Christianity; (2) inhumanity, oppression, and nonviolence; (3) openness to experience; and (4) relational climate and actualization.

"Religious belief in action": An existential Christianity

Right from the first entry on February 15th, Carl provided a theme that would become more developed over the course of the trip, and in some ways the course of his life. Carl wrote,

> Our religion is worse than useless, if it is only a negative thing, for by its very nature it ought to be the most positive and compelling force in our lives. According to my firm conviction, it doesnt make much difference what we do not believe, even though it is an old church doctrine, but it does make a tremendous difference what we DO believe, and believe in strongly enough to make our lives conform to our beliefs.

In other words, faith and religion are best when lived, when acted upon. Christianity is not a spectator sport, nor an allegiance to dogma; it is the actualization of what one believes is true, ethical, and transcendent. It is a consistency between one's ideals and one's actions. On February 26th, Rogers named and valued a similar theme in John Mott's sermon of that day, writing "our spiritual life is the result of exercise, just as the development of our physical and intellectual life is the result of exercise." It is apparent within the first days of his trip that Carl prizes this idea of living "out" what one believes "in."

The conception of Christianity as a consistent practice more than a belief system becomes further refined during his journey, developing into a genuine consistency of thoughts, feelings, and actions. On April 10th, he wrote of the importance that we must "live our Christianity." He discussed the importance of being "wide awake," which to him meant that a person honestly searches for the "Truth," "hates any form of hypocrisy," and is willing to "frankly discuss" any situation, being "highly critical" to not "swallow anything whole," and not "evade the facts." These ideas foreshadow the central person-centered concept of congruence and its facets of self-awareness, transparence and extensionality. Rogers seemed to be implying that one needs to have ideals, be aware of how one is or is not meeting them, be honest about that and engage with the world and its many perspectives and problems to live "wide awake" as a Christian.

As Carl matured during his trip this theme became increasingly humanistic or "in-the-world," a transition which might be characterized by his phrase "Christianizing the Social Order" (April 6th). On April 3rd discussing April 1st, Carl wrote, "for if we begin to live out Jesus' principles along one line, we will undoubtably begin along other lines, and then the revolutionizing of the world will begin." He seemed to believe that faith should lead not just to one's relationship with God or one's relationship with individuals but to broader social interactions. Rogers seemed to go so far as to separate the need for faith in the divinity of scripture from living out the loving values of Christianity. For example, on June 20th he writes about the plight of women and girls, some as young as six and seven, who are working in a silk factory:

> Anyone who could see those little kids, and say that such things were all right, is not a Christian, by my definition. I dont care whether he believes the whole Bible from beginning to end or whether he believes every orthodox doctrine that ever was – I wouldnt call him a Christian.

By July 17th in describing July 11th, Carl discusses the concept of social guilt and responsibility, further pushing the envelope of social justice Christianity: "<u>You</u> are partly responsible for those conditions … yet <u>you</u> let them do it."

Carl seemed to be considering that living a truly Christian life means being open to seeing the real world, taking a social stand, and working against inhumanity for reforms. Rogers spent considerable time listening and talking about pacifism and war with people from a variety of cultures and political roles. He lived through World War I, the (first) Chinese revolution, and the build up to armed conflicts in Korea, China, and other places. He also described inhumane work conditions and a variety of successful and unsuccessful leadership styles. Carl seemed to be moving towards the notion that nonviolence, and its accompanying philosophy of influence, seems most consistent with Christianity and that this consistency is vital for a true and mature life of faith.

"We are sitting on a pent up volcano": Inhumanity, oppression, and nonviolence

Immediately upon arrival in Asia, before he even got off the boat, Rogers was sensitive to the inhumanity of labor conditions he observed. He was preoccupied with the rickshaws of Tokyo, writing about them multiple times, and was particularly concerned about the dehumanizing quality of the work,

> It is a queer feeling to ride behind a human draft animal. It is something that I am afraid I would never get used to ... I couldnt help but think of the fact that he was a man, not an animal, and that he had a home, no doubt, and possibly a family, and – well, I dont know that I can describe it, but the idea of having a man lower himself to the position of draft animal in order to pull you around, is not pleasant. (March 12)

The "Calendar" and "Diary" show that it is after his arrival in Japan that Carl begins to write consistently about his concern with indignity, oppression and persons' roles in these issues.

Carl expressed concerns that seem to foreshadow some of the globalization and human rights concerns still relevant in China and Korea today. On March 18th, Carl wrote:

> Of course with the bringing in of the American industrial system, comes the American greed for money, and the exploitation of the people. I wonder if Japan will have to go thru the long fight for the reasonable rights of labor that America has had to go thru.

On April 3rd referring to March 31st, he wrote about Chinese student critics who asserted how Christianity can be seen as part of a capitalist problem and an oppressive force. His reaction was largely one of valuing and openness: "They are putting up a real fight, and I have no doubt it will eventually be a good thing." He was concerned about oppression between cultures, referring to Japanese "suppression" in relation to Korea: "we are sitting on a pent up volcano" (March 23), but his solution is to bring Christian values of brotherhood to bear: "Naturally, in trying to follow out the principles of Jesus, the Christians have come in conflict with the powers that be" (March 24). On April 3rd, how existential faith and addressing the ills of the world are intimately related is better expressed,

> The whole discussion was tremendously interesting, and I couldnt help but feel that we are right on the brink of a new Christian era, when we are going to quit, perhaps theologising about Christ, and begin to really practise his principles.

Carl seemed to have some recognition of the negative effects of cultural interaction between more powerful and less powerful groups, as well as the effects that organizing and frank discussion reveal and provide opportunities for healing.

On May 17th, Carl described a concern that remained with him throughout his life, and became more prominent in his final decade in the 1980s, a concern with the longevity of humanity. He wrote:

> it certainly gives a person a chance to wonder if after all, civilization as we know it may not be headed for extinction within the next couple of generations. I tell you, the world is not going to take up the Christian method of settling disputes between nations because

it wants to, but because it is going to be suicide if it doesnt. (May 17)

Such apocalyptic possibility and its potential solutions remained a concern of Rogers throughout his life, through World War II, the Cold War, and numerous other armed and unarmed conflicts. In addition to a way of interacting, he sees a special role for personal responsibility, at least for himself:

> I wish I knew why I am always so lucky. It seems as if I were always on the inside, by some hook or crook or accident, whenever there is anything of real interest going on. I am having opportunities that competent men would give a years pay to have. Yet they just fall into my hands. It means a big responsibility. (May 17)

It is astounding how Rogers at both age 20 and age 80 engaged in large-scale peace projects, interacting in some of the most conflictual hotspots with world leaders. But it is not only Rogers' luck to be in special places, but his open approach that made them special.

"A tremendous panorama": Openness to experience

Rogers was an agriculture student at the University of Wisconsin at the time he traveled to China. He grew up in part on a farm, loved the woods and study of animals and was from an early age an astute observer of nature. When Carl was 13, he was passionately absorbed in the study of moths; breeding, and cataloging them, and following them through their 12-month life cycle (Kirschenbaum, 2007, p. 12). He was open to beauty and had a fascination with nature. His appreciation for the Far

East was not limited however to the natural surroundings, but also the cultural and most especially the relational and the self-discovery that ensued.

Carl was absorbed in the beauty and people of places with a perpetual interest in what was to come. In describing the hills around Kyoto, he wrote, "One can't help but sort of absorb a sense of power from their splendid strength" (March 16). I get the sense that this might describe much of his life – an openness to the power, or potential power, in everyone and everything. Carl was a bit of an optimist and always looking towards what would unfold. Two days into his journey, on February 17th, he wrote, "tomorrow will undoubtably be even more beautiful than today." Carl had an attitude of curiosity and receptivity, especially for what could emerge in interactions. Just after visiting the Taoist Temple of Heaven in Peking (Beijing), Carl wrote, "People are the real thing" (March 27). Despite little progress for days in meetings at the World Conference, "We didnt get anywhere," Carl kept persevering with openness to what might emerge, hoping for a "spiritual unity deeper than our differences" (April 10). Likewise, he did not get disgusted or disappointed, on the contrary, he was motivated to live out his faith, being "willing … to fail" in "putting the spirit of Christ" in endeavors. As he observed inhumane work and living conditions, he wrote, "what we need are managers who see so many thousand human personalities, every one of them with great possibilities" (April 21). Even at this youthful age, Rogers was open to the breadth of experience and its inherent potential to become.

The "plot" of the diary has its climax while Carl is absorbed in nature in his climb of Mt. Fuji described in the July 27th entry. In his first entry on landing in Japan, he mentioned Mt. Fuji. He admired it, though he could not see it at all upon arrival, almost longed for it, wanting "to see Fuji as we steamed into the harbor" (March 12). Then on March 15th, he wrote "I peered ahead, and all of a sudden my breath kind of stopped, for there, there, there, was Fuji!" His initial reaction was like an ineffable peak experience of openness:

> All that I can say about it is that even after all the pictures we have seen of it, and all the paintings, Fuji itself was no disappointment. It was better than the best picture of it I have ever seen, and that is as far as I can go in trying to describe it. (March 15)

When he returned to Japan in July, as nearly the last action in the Orient, he wrote "I realized it was up to me" to climb Mt. Fuji. Despite this initiative and self-reliant flair, Carl valued those who climbed with him, "Luck was with me, and I picked up two nice chaps." Carl made the decision to climb, and even when his friend and mentor (Princeton Professor Ken LaTourette) was too ill, that climb was supported by the folks he met at the start and fellow "pilgrims" along the way. In the middle of the night, he decided he needed to leave his fellow travelers in order to make the summit by daybreak and went ahead on his own. During the peak experience at the summit as the sun rose, Carl comments less on his own pride than on the relational resonance of the experience:

> I wish you could have heard the shout that came from the many pilgrims at various stages of the climb, when the sun finally shoved its white-hot brim up thru those soft white clouds. And I shouted too, and waved my cap. We had seen a tremendous event. (July 27)

It is this interconnected appreciation of the individual's actualization and the relational climate that releases and fosters it, that became the central theme of his life's work.

"Hammering out our faith in the forge of discussion": Relational climate and actualization

Perhaps Carl's most enduring idea is that when provided with a facilitative relational climate characterized by empathy, warmth, and genuineness, persons grow and change in beneficial ways. *The China Diary* reveal that same theme for his own identity development. From the first week, he is anticipating his interactions with his traveling cohort and over and over again in the diary he asserts that he can't get enough of his discussions with others. He uses the word "discussion" 23 times and on many of these they are accompanied by gratitude or interest. For example, on February 25th, Carl wrote, "We have had many discussions already on lots of the doubtful points and I am thankful beyond words." In fact in using the phrase, "this was really a high spot" Carl is not referring to his climb of Mt. Fuji but to his love of a discussion (April 3). On March 5th, he wrote, "We are literally hammering out our faith in the forge of discussion. It surely is great." And on February 25th, he wrote, "The more we talk and think, the more I am finding it possible to define what I myself believe, and what I consider non-essential." How to create life, how to "become" through existential faith is in the warmth and strength of cooperative interaction with others. He seems to express the most value for those deep, ongoing relationships he has with those with whom he is traveling and can speak and listen fully. But it is not just on serious issues that Carl bonds. He consistently shows a sense of humor and a playful spirit:

we had "more fun than a box of monkeys" (February 24).

Clearly, there is a core group of fellow travelers that provide a facilitative learning climate for Carl. However, Carl's relational climate also includes those to whom he is writing day after day and those with whom he has only days or hours to interact. This total relational milieu helps influence his "becoming." The "Cast of Characters" chapter gives a short glimpse of the breadth and depth of his relationships while traveling. In his youth like in his final years, Carl was engaging with world leaders for peace. For example, concerning April 8, he wrote, "I would have liked to differ again with the Ex Chancellor of the German Empire. He and I had a hard time agreeing, all the way thru" (April 10).

He wrote frequently to his parents, his future wife Helen, and others in the USA. For example, on February 27, well into his trip across the Pacific, he wrote, "Part of the morning I wrote letters, but I had finished most of the seventeen the evening before, so that I spent the greater part of the time up on deck, watching the sights." It is this depth of prolonged, reflective interaction and breadth that provided him a rich soil in which to grow. In the final entry, Carl concludes the diary anticipating that his "job" will be to:

> get the men to think – and when I have gotten them to thinking a little bit, then to get them to think some more – and some more! Most of us have never thought our way thru to find out what the real purpose of a YM should be. (July 30)

Carl seems to not only be alluding to the purpose of the YMCA, but also to the purpose of his life, or life in general. He is foreshadowing what he will articulate later in life as the purpose of humanistic education and the vitality of extensional critical thinking and perspective taking. He recapitulates that he wants to "make men thoroly uncomfortable, to drag them out and make them think." While clearly the directive, confrontational nature of "uncomfortable" and "drag" are not characteristic of the mature Rogers, but the frank person-to-person dialogue is. Likewise, the unerring desire remains, the desire to live out faith in the world and confront experience openly to pursue all of one's potential purpose.

In the final paragraph of the diary, Carl provides the only reference to his interactions with the important religious philosopher W. B. Sharman, calling him "the most stimulating man I have ever been with." Carl rarely writes in the diary near the end of his trip, and it is clear that he and Sharman are traveling together and interacting daily during the weeks it takes to cross the Pacific. How much more could he have said about how his ideas were evolving at the end of the diary? I guess I am drawn again and again to the little phrase, "I have ever been with." The idea of "being-with" is central to the essence of the person-centered approach. I am glad Carl left us this intimate look at his life during this important odyssey across the world and into himself at the dawn of his adulthood.

In a letter written home, probably in early August, Carl wrote,

> Naturally all of these friendships, and this eye-opening trip, and the time to think that I have had on shipboard, etc., have tremendously changed me. Most of all perhaps, I have changed to the only logical viewpoint – that I want to know what is true, regardless of whether that leaves me a Christian or no. Since taking this attitude (and it has been a gradual step, starting before

I left home) I have found the most wonderful new riches in the life of Christ and in the Bible as a whole. (Kirschenbaum, 2007, p. 25)

One might draw many conclusions from this passage, but the one that stays with me is how a relational climate, "all these friendships," lead him to have changed to an attitude of openness, towards "what is true," and thereby "have found the most wonderful new riches" in life. In other words, the highly influential person-centered narrative – that a facilitative relational climate characterized by grace leads towards the fully functional person – seems to have taken place in Carl's own life long before he found the words for it.

REFERENCES

Anderson, G. H. (1999). Kenneth Scott LaTourette. *Biographical dictionary of Christian missionaries.* Grand Rapids, MI: Edermans.

Cornelius-White, J. H. D., & Harbaugh, A. P. (2010). *Learner-centered instruction: Building relationships for student success.* Thousand Oaks, CA: Sage.

Cornelius-White, J. H. D., & Motschnig-Pitrik, R. (2010). Effectiveness beyond psychotherapy: The person-centered, experiential paradigm in education, parenting, and management. In M. Cooper, J. Watson, & D. Hölldampf (Eds.), *Person-centered and experiential therapies work: A review of the research on counseling, psychotherapy and related practices* (pp. 45–64). Ross-on-Wye, UK: PCCS Books.

Hopkins, C. H. (1979). *John R. Mott, 1865–1955: A biography.* Grand Rapids, MI: Eerdmans.

Hutchings, G. (2001). *Modern China: A guide to a century of change.* Cambridge, MA: Harvard University Press.

Kirschenbaum, H. (1979). *On becoming Carl Rogers.* New York: Delacorte/Delta.

Kirschenbaum, H. (2007). *The life and work of Carl Rogers.* Ross-on-Wye, UK: PCCS Books.

Psychotherapy Networker. (2007, March/April). The top 10: The most influential therapists of the past quarter-century. Retrieved July 15, 2011 from http://www.psychotherapynetworker.org/populartopics/leaders-in-the-field/219

Rogers, C. R. (1922, June). An experiment in Christian internationalism. *The Intercollegian, 9,* 1–2.

Rogers, C. R. (1951). *Client-centered therapy.* Boston: Houghton Mifflin.

Rogers, C. R. (1959. A theory of therapy, personality, and interpersonal relationships, as developed in the client-centered framework. In S. Koch (Ed.), *Psychology: A study of a science. Vol. 3: Formulations of the person and the social context* (pp 184–256). New York: McGraw-Hill.

Rogers, C. R. (1961). *On becoming a person: A therapist's view of psychotherapy.* Boston: Houghton Mifflin.

Rogers, C. R. (1968). *Journey into self* [Motion picture, W. H. McGaw Jr., Producer]. UCLA Extension Media Center.
Rogers, C. R. (1969). *Freedom to learn: A view of what education might become.* Columbus, OH: Charles E. Merrill.
Rogers, C. R. (1977). *On personal power: Inner strength and its revolutionary impact.* New York: Delacorte.
Rogers, C. R. (1980). *A way of being.* Boston: Houghton Mifflin.
Rogers, C. R. (1983). *Freedom to learn for the 80s.* Columbus, OH: Charles E. Merrill.
Rogers, C. R., & Freiberg, H. J. (1994). *Freedom to learn* (3rd ed.). Columbus, OH: Charles E. Merrill.
Rogers, C. R., Gendlin, E. T., Kiesler, D. J., & Truax, C. B. (1967). *The therapeutic relationship and its impact: A study of psychotherapy with schizophrenics.* Madison, WI: University of Wisconsin Press.
Rogers, C. R., & Russell, D. (2002). *Carl Rogers: The quiet revolutionary: An oral history.* Roseville, CA: Penmarin Books.
Rogers, N. (2003). *Carl Roger: A daughter's tribute* [CD-ROM]. Marina Del Rey, CA: Mindgarden Media.
Setran, D. P. (2007). *The college Y: Student religion in the era of secularization.* New York: Palgrave MacMillan.
Sherer, R. G. (n.d.) King, Willis Jefferson. *Handbook of Texas Online.* Retrieved July 15, 2011, from http://www.tshaonline.org/handbook/online/articles/fki56. Published by the Texas State Historical Association.
Thorne, B. (2003). *Carl Rogers* (2nd ed.). London: Sage.

INDEX

A
Alcatraz Island, California 27, 32
Aleutian Islands 170
America 1, 7, 96,
American Psychological Association xi
Amoy (Xiamen), China 148, 189
Anderson, GH 15
Andrews, Roy Chapman 150
Antipolo, Philippines 132
anti-religion movement, China 93
Antung, Korea 82
Asano, Mr. 52
Australia 96, 100

B
Baker, Mr. 146
Baptist 143, 145
Beijing, China iii, 2, 184, 185 (see also Peking)
Berkeley, California 27, 28, 181
Bidgrain, Mlle. 95
Blue Canyon, California 25
Bolshevism 104, 156
Boss, Miss 166
Bozarth, Jerold 4
Brockman, Fletcher 101
Buddha, Daibutsu 69, 183
Buddhism 67, 69, 82, 150, 151, 162, 169, 183, 191
Bulgaria 91, 96

Bull, Mr. 96

C
Canada 16, 96
Canton, China iii, 136, 137, 138, 142, 143, 146, 187, 188, 189
Canton Christian College 136, 188
Case, Austin 17, 32, 33, 35, 41, 54, 58, 73
Catholicism 133, 134
Center for the Studies of the Person (CSP), California 4, 5
Chang Chien 158, 160
Chang Tso Lin, General 83, 107, 111, 183
Chen, Mr. 106
Cheng, Dr. 123
Chengchow, China 112, 114, 117, 187
Cheyenne, Wyoming 24
Chicago ii, v, vi, 1, 4, 24
Chicago Counseling Center 3
Chien-Men Gate, China 87
Childs, John Lawrence "Jack" 18, 84, 86, 89
China 82*ff passim*
Chou, Colonel 110
Chowchowfu (Chaozhou), China 143, 144, 145, 146, 147, 189, 190
Christ 27, 41, 92, 94, 95, 101, 104, 105, 114, 124, 199

Christianity 67, 79, 80, 92, 93,100, 103, 132, 156, 157, 160, 161, 162, 185, 195–7, 199
Claremont, California 181
Colorado 23
Confucianism 92, 121, 144, 186
Confucius 121, 144, 186
Conrad, Dean 33, 127
Cornelius-White, Jeffrey xi, xiv, 4, 178, 195
Corpus, Mr. 130
Council Bluffs, Iowa 23
Cressey/Cressy, Paul 102, 147, 166
Cyn, Mr. 78, 79, 80
Czechoslovakia 96

D
Daibutsu Buddha 69, 183
Dakota 23
Das, Maya 95, 98, 102
Denton, Florence, school for girls 68
Dewey, Commodore 128
Dewey, John 3, 18
Diamond Head, Hawaii 42
Doshisha school, Kyoto, Japan 68

E
East Asia 7
Ellen, Glen vi
Elliott, Helen x, 2, 10, 18*ff*, 19, 37, 148
England 96, 157

F
Fan, Miss 95
Foochow (Fuzhou), China 147, 149, 150, 178, 189, 190, 191
Foochow College 149

Forbidden City, Peking, China 86, 88, 184
Fort McKinley, Philippines 130
France 7
Fujiyama (see Mt. Fuji)
Fukien Christian University, China 150
Fusan, Korea 73, 74, 183
Fuzhou, (Foochow) China 178, 209

G
Gailey, Mr. 86
Gale, Mr, 165
Galland, Mr. 95
Garrett, Dr. 158
Gartrell, David xiv
Geldart, John Hays 18, 123, 125, 126, 153, 162, 163, 165
Gendlin, Eugene 4
George, Katy Boyd 33, 37, 40, 47, 54, 57
Germany 17, 96
Gandhi, Mahatma 94
Goat Island, California 32
God 30, 87, 103, 104
Golden Gate Park, California 30
Goodrich, Mrs. 101
Gotemba, Japan 170, 192
Grafton, Mr. 70
Grand Canal, China 162, 163
Grand Island, Nebraska 24
Great Salt Lake, Utah 24
Great Wall, The, China 98
Greece 96
Grover, Prof. 68

H
Hall, Mr. 106, 110, 116
Han River, China 143

INDEX

Hangchow, China 162, 164, 165, 191
Hangchow College 164
Hankow, China 111, 114, 115, 119, 186
Hankow Y 116
Hannon, Wade xiv
Hanyang Iron Works 116, 187
Harbaugh, AP 4
Harlow, Mr. 101
Hawaii xiii, 8, 183
Hayes, Mr. 155, 165
Heim, Prof. 98, 106, 110
Hemingway, Dr. 107
Henry, Mr. 136
Higashi Honganji temple, Japan 63
Hildreth, Mr. 146, 147
Hinduism 92
Hodgkin, HT 18, 71, 97, 98, 101, 102
Holland 96
Hong Kong, China iii, 7, 136, 141, 143, 186, 188, 189
Honolulu, Hawaii 42, 183
Hoto waterfalls, Japan 57
Houghton, Mr. 138
Hsiakwan, China 160, 191
Hutchings, G 7, 9

I

Imperial University, Kyoto, Japan 50, 64, 67
India 100
Iowa 23

J

Japan v, xiii, 7, 8, 15, 23, 47, 48*ff*, 78, 88, 95, 183, 198
Japanese University, Shanghai, China 126
Jesus 16, 41, 94, 196

Johnson, Lydia 34, 35, 37, 40, 42
Johnston, Colonel 133
Jorgenson, (Jorgy) Mr. 49, 51
Jorgenson, Mrs. 53
Judaism 92

K

Kamys, Judge 134
Kasbeer, Helen 17, 32, 34
Kato, Baron 39, 48, 66
Kawai, Miss 95
Kelly, Miss 153
Kennedy, Jean 26, 32, 34, 73
Kichang River, China 143
Kiesler, DJ 4
Kilpatrick, William Heard 3
King, Willis J 11, 13, 32, 33, 37, 41, 63, 95, 125, 126, 127, 181
Kiomidzu temple, Japan 63
Kirschenbaum, Howard xi, xii, xiii, xv, 1, 19, 200, 206
Klavin, Miss 91, 96
Kobashi, Mr. 169
Kobe, Japan 64, 65, 70, 72, 183
Koch, Pastor 4, 98
Kokchea, China 144
Koo, Mr. 90, 92
Korea v, xiii, 7, 8, 18, 73*ff*, 183, 197, 199
Korean Y 78
Kulangsu Island, China 148
Kushan (mountain), china 149, 150, 152, 191
Kwannon, Goddess of Mercy 63
Kwong, Mr. Wong 117
Kyoto, Japan 62, 63, 64, 68, 70, 183, 201

211

L

La Jolla, California 4
Langshan (mountain), China 159
LaTourette, Kenneth Scott 11, 14, 31, 33, 35, 36, 37, 81, 82, 135, 140, 141, 143, 148, 166, 170, 174, 181, 202
Laubach, Dr. 130
League of Nations 47, 95
Lee, Frank 137
Lerigo, Mr. 188
Lew, Dr. 90, 92
Li Yuan Hung 141, 142
Lodge, Sir Oliver 27
Luccock, Emory 163
Luzon Island, Philippines 128, 187

M

Macao, China 139
MacConnell, Mr. 149
Macklin, Dr. 160, 161
Magee, Mr. 160
Makteer Girls School, China 125
Manchuria 8, 83, 183
Manila, Philippines 123, 142, 187
Manila Harbor, Philippines 128
Mary Johnstone Hospital, Manila, Philippines 129
Medard, Mr. 106, 109
Meiji shrines, Japan 169, 192
Melby, Eva 149
Michaelis, Dr. 17, 98, 101
Min River, China 148, 189
Mitani, Mr. 47
Mokanshan, China 162, 163, 191
Moncrieff, Miss 94
Monet, Capt. 98

Mongolia 8
Monnier, Prof. 98, 102
Motschnig-Pitrik, R xi
Mott, John 5, 6, 11, 12, 16, 21, 27, 29, 31, 33, 24, 37, 40, 41, 43, 47, 53, 66, 83, 85, 95, 96, 97, 102, 181, 183, 184, 185, 196
Mott, Mrs. 37
Mt. Fuji, Japan iii, 59, 61, 170, 173, 180, 192, 193, 201, 202, 203
Mukden, China 82, 83, 183
Munsen, Mr. & Mrs. 149, 150
Muskrat, Ruth 34, 46, 127

N

Nagasaki, Japan 167, 192
Nakagawa, our waiter 40
Nanking, China 120, 121, 160, 186, 187, 191
Nankow Pass, China 98
Nantunchow, China 158, 191
Nara, Japan 64, 68, 69, 183
Nara Park, Japan 69
Nash, Mr. 75
National Christian Conference of China 123–5, 187
Neff, Mr. 150
New York 3
New Zealand 96
Nikitin, Mr. 91
Nikko, Japan 54, 55, 56, 57, 58, 63, 183
Niwa, Mr. 75, 78
North Gate Tower, Foochow, China 149
North Platte, Nebraska 23
Northern Ireland 5

INDEX

O

Oahu Island, Hawaii 42
Oak Park, Ilinois 1
Oakland, California 26, 27, 181
Oberlin Shansi Mission, China 108
Omaha, Nebraska 23
Osaka, Japan 65
Osakusa Temple, Japan 169
Otto, Mr. 159

P

Pacifism 94, 100, 101, 185
pagodas 148, 159, 162, 165, 191, 152
Pagoda anchorage, China 148, 149, 152, 189, 190
Patterson, Mr. 50
Paul, Mr. x, 92, 95, 101, 102, 165
Pearl Harbor, Hawaii 43
Peking, China vi, 2, 78, 84, 86, 107, 178, 184, 185, 201 (see also Beijing)
Peking Union Medical College 84, 89
Phelps, Mrs. 49, 51, 53
Philippines xiii, 18, 96, 128, 133, 186
Phillips, Cecil 106, 116
Platte River, Nebraska 23
Poland 96
Port Acosta, California 26
Porter, David R 3, 6, 11, 13, 27, 30, 31, 32, 33, 37, 41, 43, 50, 54
Purple Mountain, China 122

Q

Quakerism 71, 101

R

Robinson, Mr. 101

Rochester, New York xiv, 3
Rogers, Walter (father) 21
Rogers, Natalie (daughter) xii, xiv, 3
Ross, Prof. 22
Rugh, Arthur 43
Rugh, Dwight 43
Russell, D xii, xiii, 14, 16, 17, 18, 19
Russia 7, 8, 91, 96, 99
Rust, Austria 5
Rutgers, Dr. 33, 90, 96

S

Saito, Mr. 51
San Francisco, California ii, v, 8, 13, 27, 32, 181
Sanjusangendo temple, Japan 63
Santos, Judge 132, 133
Seaman, Mrs. 165
Seiyoken Hotel, Japan 50
Seoul, Korea iii, 75, 76, 183
Seoul, Mayor of 18
Setran, DP 5, 6, 7, 12, 13
Shanghai, China iii, 92, 123, 127, 152, 162, 165, 179, 184, 190, 191
Shanghai Baptist College 125, 152, 187, 190
Sharman, Henry Burton 10, 11, 15, 174, 193, 205
Shedd, Mr. 118
Sheminoseki, Japan 73, 183
Sherman, Miss 33, 37, 42
Shiba Park, Japan 50
Shikiachuang, China 106, 111, 187
Shintoism 67
Sikhism 188
Smith, Miss 147
Smith, Mr. 112

213

Soochow, China 161, 162, 191
South Africa 5, 96
Spain 128
Steinmetz, Dr. 128, 129
Stockwell, Mr. 41
Subashiri, Japan 171
Summer Palace, China 97
Sun Yat-sen 138, 141
Swatow (Shantou), China 9, 143, 166, 189
Sweetman, Mrs. 120, 121
Switzerland 95
Szeged, Hungary 5

T
Tai, Mr. 165
Taiku, China 107, 108, 185
Taiyuanfu, China iii, 106, 185, 187
Taoism 201
Tate, Dr. 81
Tchou, Mr. 157
Temple of Heaven, Peking, China 86, 88, 169, 184
Thorne, Brian xii
Tingley, Mildred 34, 35, 37, 40, 42, 73
Togo, Admiral 39, 48
Tokyo, Japan ii, iii, 50, 52, 53, 58, 59, 63, 64, 65, 66, 167, 169, 182, 183, 192, 198
Truax, CB 4
Truckee, California 25
Tsing Hua College, China 97, 184
Tung Wen College, China 153
Tungchow, China 159
Turner, Mr. 128, 131, 135

U
Uet Hsu, China 107, 109, 185
Union Theological Seminary, New York 3
University, Boone 119
University of California Santa Barbara xiii, xiv, 20
University of Chicago 3
University of Chicago Divinity School 16
University, Columbia 3, 18
University, Imperial, Kyoto, Japan 50, 64, 67
University, Japanese, Shanghai, China 126
University, Missouri State xiv
University of Nanking, China 121, 122
University, Ohio State 3, 33
University, Southeastern 121
University of Wisconsin vi, 2, 3, 4, 200
USSR 5
Utah 25, 181
Uyeno Park, Japan 50

W
Wang, CT 141
Watanabe, Chief Justice, of Korea 18, 78
Wemura, Dr. 52
Western Behavioral Sciences Institute, California 4
Wheaton, Illinois 22, 181
Wilson, Keith xiv, 178
Wisconsin 17
Wolf, Dad 29
Wolfe, Mr. 64
Wong, Tom 165

214

Wood, Leonard, Governor General of
 the Philippines 17, 18, 133, 188
Woosung, China 192
Wu Pei Fu 107, 111, 141, 142
Wuchang, China 115, 119, 186
Wyoming 181

Y

Y 67, 126 (see also YMCA)
 Chinese 86, 89, 90, 102, 110, 112,
  114, 116, 126, 139, 157
 Japanese 51, 67
  in Korea 78
 Korean 78, 79
 Philippine 128, 130
Yale Divinity School 15, 36
Yangtze Engineering Works, China 116,
 117, 118, 186
Yen, Governor 109
Yenping, China 150
YMCA (Young Men's Christian Association) vi, ix, x, xiii, 2, 5–7, 9,
 11, 12, 13, 18, 151, 162, 191,
 204 (see also Y)
YM Commercial College, Peking, China
 84
Yokohama, Japan 46, 58, 70, 166, 170,
 182, 192
Yuasa, Mr. 57
Yui, David 102
Yun, Baron 80

Z

Zachariah, Miss 95, 115, 116
Zung, Mr. 112

THE LIFE AND WORK OF CARL ROGERS
Howard Kirschenbaum

ISBN 978 1 898059 98 1
pp 736, £50.00 (cloth cover with dust jacket)
ISBN 978 1 898059 93 6
pp 736, £27.00 (hardback)
Discounts from www.pccs-books.co.uk

This extended and revised second edition of Kirschenbaum's acclaimed biography includes a more detailed personal and professional history, and a full account of the last decade of Rogers' life. That decade turned out to be one of the most important periods of his career in which he developed peace work in many places in the world, including South Africa and Northern Ireland, culminating in a Nobel Peace Prize nomination just days before his death. Until now this work has not been widely known.

The new edition adds deeper understanding of Rogers' contributions to psychology, the helping professions and society. On a personal level, access to recently revealed private papers tells us much more about Carl Rogers the man than was known to many of his closest associates. Kirschenbaum reflects a wiser and more balanced perspective of his subject; and now fully referenced, this is *The Life and Work of Carl Rogers*.

REVIEWS

I couldn't put it down. I kept jumping from one part of the book to another and getting absorbed in the close research and the wonderful detail. I know the book took years to research, and now I can see why. Even reading the footnotes is absorbing.
Professor Dave Mearns, ex University of Strathclyde

This book is the definitive biography of this leading figure whose influence in contemporary society extends so much further than person-centred therapy and psychology for which he is best known.
Tim Bond, Professor in the School of Education, University of Bristol. Past Chair of the British Association for Counselling (BAC)

Howard Kirschenbaum, Ed.D., is Professor Emeritus and former Chair of Counseling and Human Development, Warner Graduate School of Education and Human Development, University of Rochester, New York. He is a leading interpreter of the life and work of Carl Rogers, and author of the earlier biography *On Becoming Carl Rogers*, co-editor of *The Carl Rogers Reader* and *Carl Rogers: Dialogues*, and writer and producer of the best-selling DVD, *Carl Rogers and the Person-Centered Approach*.